THE
BOAT
DRINKS
BOOK

Adlard Coles Nautical
An imprint of Bloomsbury Publishing Plc

50 Bedford Square   1385 Broadway
London   New York
WC1B 3DP   NY 10018
UK   USA

www.bloomsbury.com
www.adlardcoles.com

ADLARD COLES, ADLARD COLES
NAUTICAL and the Buoy logo are
trademarks of Bloomsbury Publishing Plc

First published 2017

© Fiona Sims, 2017

Illustrations © Louise Sheeran
Photographs © Julian Winslow,
except where credited otherwise

British Library Cataloguing-in-
Publication Data

A catalogue record for this book is
available from the British Library.

Library of Congress Cataloguing-in-
Publication data has been applied for.
ISBN: 978-1-4729-3065-1
ePDF: 978-1-4729-3066-8
ePub: 978-1-4729-3067-5

10 9 8 7 6 5 4 3 2 1

Typeset in Leander by Austin Taylor
Printed and bound in China by
 Toppan Leefung Printing

Bloomsbury Publishing Plc makes
every effort to ensure that the papers
used in the manufacture of our books
are natural, recyclable products made
from wood grown in well-managed
forests. Our manufacturing processes
conform to the environmental
regulations of the country of origin.

To find out more about our authors
and books visit www.bloomsbury.com.
Here you will find extracts,
author interviews, details of
forthcoming events and the
option to sign up for our newsletters.

Steady as she goes

Now this is the bit where I point
out that while you are hopefully
enjoying the book you should also
be consuming alcohol responsibly
– and in port, preferably.
Boating and drinking is fun,
we know, but too much of one,
while doing the other? Not so
much. www.drinkaware.co.uk

THE BOAT DRINKS BOOK

A different tipple
in every port

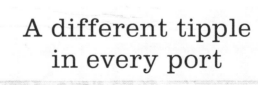

FIONA SIMS

ADLARD COLES NAUTICAL

BLOOMSBURY

LONDON · OXFORD · NEW YORK · NEW DELHI · SYDNEY

Contents

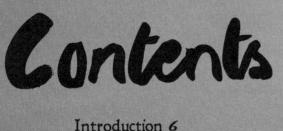

Introduction 6

Kitting Out 10

Kit 12
Locker 15

Atlantic 22

England, South Coast 24
  NIBBLE *Potted shrimps* 28
Scotland 30
Holland 31
Channel Islands 32
France, West Coast 34
  NIBBLE *Artichoke, feta and ham tart* 38
Spain, North and West Coast 40
Portugal 42
  NIBBLE *Sardine-stuffed eggs* 44
Canaries 46
US, East Coast 47
Florida Keys 48
  NIBBLE *Black bean salsa* 50
South Africa 52

Med 54

France, South Coast 56
  NIBBLE *Two-olive tapenade* 58
Corsica 60
Italy 62
  NIBBLE *Black polenta, sun-dried tomato and mozzarella* 66
Spain 68
  NIBBLE *Tuna-stuffed piquillo peppers* 70
Croatia and Montenegro 72
Greece 74
  NIBBLE *Feta and olive bites* 76
Turkey 78

Baltic 80

Denmark 82
Germany 84
Sweden 86
  NIBBLE *Gravadlax and beetroot* 88
Russia 90

Pacific 92

Australia 94
New Zealand 99
  NIBBLE *Stuffed mussels with parsley, garlic and Parmesan* 100
Canada 102
Hong Kong 104
Singapore 106
  NIBBLE *Cheat's chicken satay* 108
US, West Coast 110

Caribbean 112

Grenada 114
British Virgin Islands 116
Barbados 118
  NIBBLE *Jerked fish skewers and chutney mayo* 120

Cocktails 122

Rum 126
Gin 132
Whisky 140
Vodka 148
Tequila 154
Non-alcoholic cocktails 160

How beer is made 167
How wine is made 168

Index 172
Acknowledgements 176

Introduction

I'm going to blame my dad once again for this book. For those who aren't familiar with *The Boat Cookbook*, which I wrote a couple of years before this one, my dad needed some help in the galley department. Out went the tinned beef stew and Smash, and in came grilled lamb chops and butter-bean mash. And he hasn't looked back. I'll go further – he's now a dab hand in the kitchen at home, fearlessly turning out new recipes. My mother, needless to say, is overjoyed.

So this time I thought I'd help to widen his knowledge about booze. I've never understood people's reluctance to learn more about the alcohol we drink – it's half the cost of the bill in restaurants, and a significant wedge of the weekly shop. We can't get enough cooking programmes and we all own the latest must-have cookbooks, yet many of us still can't make sense of a wine label. Instead, we reach for whatever is on offer, or looks most appealing.

It's true that it's difficult to find badly made booze these days (unless it's illicit hooch), such are the advances in technology, and what's wrong with own label anyway? Answer – nothing at all. But there's so much more out there to discover – and for those with a boat, even more than most.

Ok, so I've had a bit of a head start – writing about drink, as well as food, for the last 25 years, travelling the world in pursuit of brilliant winemakers, innovative distillers and craft beer nerds. In fact, I can't wait to get my hands on a small-scale producer's lovingly crafted wine/gin/ale. So I head to the nearest independent drink shop, which is invariably staffed by enthusiastic owners who can't wait to tell me about their latest finds. Or I seek out locally minded restaurants, bars and bistros that trumpet nearby producers.

I hang out in vineyards a fair bit, too, and will happily spend hours poking about in a distillery or tasting my way through a brewer's seasonal ales, yet you'll still find me drinking from a box of blush Zinfandel on board with Dad on the water on a warm summer's day. Now, there's nothing wrong with a wine box. They are perfect for stashing on board and you can buy some decent wine in a box these days. But I won't say there's nothing wrong with blush Zinfandel – let's just say that this is at the other end of the rosé spectrum that I enjoy (sorry, Dad).

So this book is for him, and for all you other boaters out there frustrated by your lack of booze knowledge but keen to know more. It's by no means a definitive guide to drinks – in fact, it misses out huge chunks of the wine world (I apologise, South America – I know you produce some stunning wines) to focus on the key sailing hubs and routes. And the book only touches on the exciting developments in recent years on craft beer, artisanal spirits *et al*, and offers just a few crumbs for the non-drinker – though I have provided some cracking booze-free cocktail recipes.

Wine dominates in this book simply because it is the most popular tipple for the boater (according to my totally unofficial poll and observations over the years) and this is where you might need the most guidance. And when I do talk about a particular country, especially when it's a major wine-producing country, I've highlighted only the key wine-producing regions that you are likely to meet in those sailing hubs – much of Europe is still rather parochial when it comes to stocking drinks outside their particular regions. But the upside of that is there's still space to recommend little jaunts away from the boat to visit particular producers, say, or to offer tips on drinking protocol when you're propping up the bar in a harbour town somewhere.

The book follows a vaguely logical course, starting on the south coast of England, darting up to Scotland, and then following the Atlantic coast from Holland down to Spain, before jumping to South Africa. I dip a toe in the Baltic and then head back to sunnier climes around the Med, skirting key coastlines and dropping by sailing hotspots, finally ending in Turkey. I also cruise the Pacific, from Australia to Singapore, and have some fun with rum in the Caribbean, before ending the book with a chapter on cocktails. Oh yes, you must have a boat cocktail.

Want to know what to eat with your boat drinks? Then I've also provided a few of my favourite boat nibble recipes, each inspired by some of the key regions I've mentioned in the book. And if you still want to reach for that box of bargain blush Zin when you've finished reading this, well, then that's fine too. You know what you like, right?

Kitting Out

The Boat Drinks Book **rule number one:** only choose the alcohol that you actually enjoy drinking – forget trying to impress guests, your galley will thank you. And start small – you're not trying to build up a home bar here. Choose the wine you like to sip, the beer you like to glug and the spirits you like to naval-gaze with. And if cocktails are your thing (and I sincerely hope they are), then only choose the ingredients needed to make the cocktails you enjoy.

I've not included any cocktail recipe that requires a blender – this book is not for posh yachts, which boast better kitchens than most of us have at home. And your average boater won't have a fridge either, just a cool box. So that means buying your ice near cocktail hour, stashing it in your cool box or ice bucket, and using it up quickly. Cheers!

Kit

Bar spoon – A long-handled spoon used to stir drinks in a mixing glass, or after serving. The 'wrong' end can be used as a muddler.

Can opener/bottle opener – Because you won't get very far without one on a boat.

Chopping board – Plastic ones, please. More hygienic.

Citrus squeezer – I love Eddington's enamel squeezers. They come in three different sizes (for oranges, lemons and limes), available from most kitchen shops.

Cocktail shaker – See page 13.

Cocktail sticks – Helpful for skewering olives in a Martini and boat nibble morsels.

Corkscrew and bottle opener – The Waiter's Friend is still my favourite, made by a company that's been going since 1945 and loved by sommeliers worldwide.

Glassware – Or I should say polycarbonate-ware, as this is what you'll probably be using on board, whatever your tipple. Polycarbonate glasses are virtually unbreakable, making them the obvious choice over other pieces of plastic glassware. They're also more lightweight than standard glasses and modern moulding techniques ensure that they come in a variety of styles. New Zealand manufacturer Strahl does fine-looking polycarbonate glasses, perfect for use on board: check out its stemless Bordeaux and Chardonnay tumblers, Champagne flutes, shot and cocktail glasses at drinkstuff.com.

Grater – Microplane fine graters are the best, available from Lakeland.co.uk.

Ice bucket – A double-insulated bucket is the way to go here; drinkstuff.com even has one with integrated tongs for a very reasonable price.

Jigger, or other spirit measure – See page 124.

Jug – Generally used for mixing larger quantities of cocktails, seek out a plastic version for the boat. Use for drinks that are to be stirred, not shaken. After stirring, the drink should be strained into a glass, or get a jug with a lid and integrated pourer, which will hold back the cubes.

SHAKING IT UP

For a bartender, the shaker is a very personal bit of kit. You learn how to handle it, grow to love it, show off with it – much like a chef does with his or her knives. For a boater, a shaker means – well, probably nothing at all. You can use a Thermos, sure. Not the old-school ones with glass inside, obviously, but the modern stainless-steel versions, which are robust enough to take a bit of a bashing. But if you're keen on cocktails, then buy a shaker for your boat.

So which shaker? If you're shaking at home, the cocktail world is your oyster; they come in all shapes and sizes, though generally there are two main types – the cobbler and the Boston shaker.

The cobbler has a built-in strainer and a small cap that fits over the lid, which makes it the easiest style of shaker to use. Seek out stainless steel as it chills the drink more quickly. Cons? The lid often isn't quite as snug as you would like it to be (especially on board) and the liquid can sneak out, sometimes spectacularly.

The Boston shaker is the bartender's choice, a two-tumbler bit of kit, one larger metal tumbler inverted over a smaller glass tumbler. But the making and breaking of the seal takes some practice, plus you need a separate strainer.

I think I've found the perfect boat cocktail shaker. American manufacturer Metrokane has developed its Rabbit Fliptop Cocktail Shaker with a double-wall construction that prevents condensation and never gets cold to the touch. But more importantly it has a leak-free pop-up top, which flips over to reveal a strainer. It cost me £30 on Amazon – the price of two cocktails in a swanky bar.

No shaker or Thermos? Use a jam jar – it shakes up cocktails a treat and doubles up as a great glass to serve your concoction in.

BOAT DRINK WISDOM

Shake the shaker as hard as you can – don't just rock it: you are trying to wake it up, not send it to sleep!
The Savoy Cocktail Book, 1930

Knife – A good paring knife is essential for making perfect slivers and twists of lemon or cucumber peel, and slices of orange. Keep it sharpened and store it safely.

Mixing glass – Use your cocktail shaker on board, or a jug for larger quantities (see above).

Muddler – Essential for pounding mint and sugar for cocktails such as a mojito – a wooden one is best, but failing that use the handle of a wooden spoon.

Pepper mill – Because freshly ground peppercorns are best.

Straws – Optional, obviously – but they look the part.

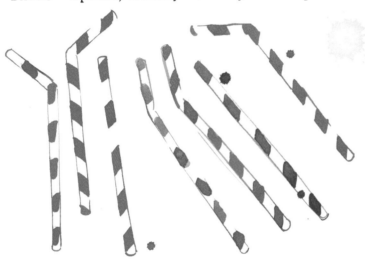

Strainer – If you don't have an integrated strainer in your cocktail shaker, you will need one that clips on to the mixing glass. Try drinkstuff.com.

Tongs – A tad more efficient than a spoon when you're trying to get ice into a glass, and they don't carry any unwanted water.

Wine preservation – My favourite on board is still the Vacu Vin Wine Saver, as it does the job just as well as newer, pricier gadgets. It extracts air from the opened bottle and reseals it with a reusable rubber stopper, slowing down the oxidation process so you can enjoy your wine at a later date. Or use a wine box, which automatically keeps the wine fresh.

A QUICK WORD ABOUT ICE

If you're intending to make a few cocktails (and let's be honest, it's hard to stop at one, especially on board), then a generous supply of ice is essential – so suss out your nearest supply. You'll need cubes of ice when shaking any drink; crushed ice, too, occasionally. To crush ice on board: wrap the cubes in a clean cloth and smash with a rolling pin. Don't have a fridge on board and want to chill your cocktail glass first? Fill each glass with crushed ice just before using and then discard. And don't be tempted to use the same ice twice when shaking cocktails.

Locker

Agave nectar – This one is for all you refined-sugar haters (that's me every now and again – I go through phases). Agave nectar is made from the juice of the agave plant – the very same used in the production of tequila. It is becoming increasingly popular in cocktails as a healthier sweetener in place of sugar syrup (see page 17) as it has a lower glycaemic index, though it is twice as sweet as sugar so the recipe needs to be adapted to allow for the additional sweetness. Available in most health food stores.

Bitters – My perfect rum punch wouldn't be the same without a dash or three of bitters. Bitters are the spice rack of the cocktail world. A liquid extraction of seeds, herbs, bark, fruit, roots, flowers and leaves, bitters are highly concentrated and used by the dash to flavour cocktails. Each brand of bitters has its own qualities that bring a unique flavour to a cocktail, and when applied judiciously they add another layer of flavour and aroma. Angostura bitters are the go-to bitters for many a bartender – boaters now, too, hopefully.

BOAT DRINK WISDOM

If all be true that I do think
There are five reasons why men drink,
Good wine, a friend, or being dry,
Or lest we should be by-and-by,
Or any other reason why.
Henry Aldrich (1647–1710)

Celery salt – I can't drink a Bloody Mary without a few grains of this flavourful condiment, which also adds interest to bog-standard tomato juice.

Coconut milk – I hold my hands up to liking Piña Colada – it's a retro classic that deserves revival.

Fruit juice – Boaters will no doubt be using long-life fruit juice – in that case, make sure you shell out for the posher brands and you will be rewarded with better-tasting drinks. Avoid anything labelled 'juice drink'. Juices to stock on board include orange, pineapple, tomato, grapefruit and apple. You'd rather use fresh juice? Squeeze it just before you want to serve your cocktails, keeping it as cool as possible until you need it. If you are making cocktails for two, then squeeze to order – the fresher the juice, the better the cocktail.

Grenadine – Essential for your Tequila Sunrise (see page 157) and Singapore Sling (see page 106) and also good in a non-alcoholic classic, the Shirley Temple (see page 162). I love Jack Rudy Small Batch Grenadine which you can buy from thewhiskyexchange.com.

Lime cordial – Rose's, preferably. For when fresh limes aren't available, and the key ingredient in a Gimlet (see page 150).

Mixers – Choose carefully: a budget tonic laced with artificial flavours and preservatives can wreck a G&T. There are a number of good mixer brands out there now to choose from – my favourite is Fever-Tree.

Nutmeg – A rum punch isn't quite the same without a light grating of nutmeg; keep a handful of whole nutmegs on board. For

grating whole nutmegs use a Microplane fine grater, mentioned previously.

Root ginger – You'll need this to make one of my all-time favourite cocktails, Gin Gin Mule, created by one of my all-time favourite bartenders, Audrey Saunders (see page 139). Also handy to quell seasickness – try adding hot water to a couple of slices of root ginger.

Salt – Maldon Salt is best.

Sugar syrup – If you like cocktails, you'll need sugar syrup to add balance. Sweetness is one of the five main tastes, along with sourness, saltiness, bitterness and umami, and it's a key component to any good drink, helping to balance acid, bitterness and alcohol. But have you ever tried to add sugar or a squeeze of honey into a cocktail mixture? Not so easy. To maximise mixing potential, sweetness ideally needs to be dissolved into syrup form. You can buy

sugar syrup (also called gomme) ready-made, of course – Monin is a popular brand stocked by many supermarkets. But failing that, it's easy to make your own: combine a mug of sugar with a mug of water in a small saucepan and dissolve over a medium heat until it thickens. Leave to cool and

decant into a bottle. Though I do have a quick cheat for you – just shake the hell out of equal parts sugar and water in a jar, let it rest a minute then shake again for 30 seconds.

Tabasco – A Bloody Mary needs a dash or two of this fiery sauce, which started life in 1868 on Avery Island in South Louisiana. The family-owned company still makes it on that very same site. Tabasco is also essential for adding a kick to freshly shucked oyster.

Worcestershire sauce – Essential in Tequila Sunrise, both Marys (Bloody and Virgin), Sangrita and a Caesar. And it elevates cheese on toast.

SEA
DOGS
ALL!

TOM
BEVAN

The
OLD
MOORINGS

THE
LONG
HAUL

A.B.C.
OF
YACHT
RACING

SAILING

THE BOAT DRINKER'S LIBRARY

On board, *The Savoy Cocktail Book* by Harry Craddock, first published in 1930. On land, turn to legendary (living) London bartender Salvatore Calabrese and his recently updated *Classic Cocktails* (Sterling Epicure). On board, *The 24-Hour Wine Expert* by the world's most respected wine critic Jancis Robinson, (Penguin), an essential guide to wine in 100 pages. On land, for something meatier turn to Jancis Robinson and Julia Harding's latest edition of *The Oxford Companion to Wine* (OUP). On board, buy *Three Sheets to the Wind: 300 bars in 13 countries – One Man's Quest for the Meaning of Beer*, by Pete Brown (Pan Macmillan). On land, *The Oxford Companion to Beer* by Brooklyn Brewery brewmaster Garrett Oliver.

Wine closures: screw cap vs. cork

Pick up a bottle of wine at your local shop and there's probably no cork in it. Plastic stoppers abound, but it's the screw cap that dominates on the wine closure front these days. No more corked or oxidised wines, say fans of the easier-to-open screw cap, who also declare that the wine invariably tastes fresher than it would do bottled under cork.

The Australians and New Zealanders were the first to start putting quality wine under screw cap. They were so fed up with the poor-quality corks they were getting from suppliers in Portugal and Spain that they set about finding an alternative closure.

So what is wrong with cork exactly? A perfect cork forms microscopic suckers that grip the bottleneck, and it's inert and impervious to liquids. But cork is a naturally occurring product and can cause two major quality issues in wine. First, a mould can develop in the bark and taint the wine, making it taste musty – this is known as 'corked' wine (see overleaf). Secondly, oxidation – because you can never produce the perfect glass cylinder inside the bottleneck, the cork can crease or split, allowing the air in, which flattens the fruit and dries out the palate.

So what does a screw cap have to offer? The top and sides are made of aluminium. Inside the top is a polyethylene liner covered with a special tin foil. The secret of the Stelvin cap, developed in the 1960s by a French manufacturer, is a foam liner with a saran-wrapped tin outer covering, which creates a neutral, airtight seal.

But screw caps aren't perfect, either. Critics moan that some wines sealed under screw cap display a 'reduced' character due to the presence of sulphur compounds, and that screw caps can sometimes mute the fruit. And the jury is still out on the effect screw caps have on older wines – we'll just to have to wait and see.

Wine faults and how to spot them

What is **corked wine**, exactly? There are (unofficial) claims that as many as one in 12 bottles of (cork-stoppered) wine are corked – which means most of us will have come across a corked bottle or three in our time. Those who can recognise the smell and taste know to give another bottle a try, but those who don't will probably never order that wine again, which is a shame. Every now and again a small amount of mould, called 2,4,6-trichloranisole or TCA, escapes the sterilisation process and remains in the cork. When the wine makes contact with the cork it soaks up the smell, hence the mouldy aroma and taste. But corkiness can happen in varying degrees – in tiny amounts, this can just dull the wine.

If that bottle of Muscadet looks a little bit more yellow than it normally does, or that young red looks a bit on the brown side, then it has probably oxidised. **Oxidation** occurs when too much air has got into the wine. And if the bottle hasn't been kept well, the cork may have dried out and shrunk a little. The wine will taste dull and flat or, in the worst case, taste of vinegar.

Then there's that nasty pong of rotten eggs you get in wine occasionally – that's **hydrogen sulphide**, which can form during fermentation, and is not to be confused with the whiff of burnt matches – sulphur dioxide – which usually clears up after the wine has been open for a bit (sulphur is usually added to the wine during bottling to keep it fresh).

Your wine is a tad cloudy? There's a growing trend for unfiltered wines, but in rare cases murky can mean a dose of **bad bacteria**. And if that old bottle of Burgundy you have been hanging on to looks a little cloudy, just let it stand upright to settle for a while, and decant if needs be, passing the last few drops through a piece of muslin.

White crystals in the bottom of your glass of white wine? They are called tartrates – they are natural deposits and won't harm you or the wine.

TEN WAYS TO CURE A HANGOVER

1 Aim for prevention. Drink a glass of milk or eat some cheese and bickies or a small pot of yoghurt before boozing – it lines the stomach and slows the absorption of alcohol.

2 Avoid a nightcap. I'm talking spirits such as whisky or brandy – they have a higher level of compounds called congeners, which are formed during the fermentation and distilling process. If you must have one, stick to white spirits. Although when it comes to having a banging head, the alcohol itself is the main culprit!

3 Alcohol causes dehydration – we all know that. So we should also know how important it is to drink a glass of water before we go to bed.

4 Make your own rehydration drink by dissolving a tablespoon of sugar and a teaspoon of salt in a pint of water and sip slowly throughout the morning.

5 Don't even think about having the hair of the dog – it's never the answer, and doesn't work anyway.

6 Keep caffeine to a minimum, it will only dehydrate you further.

7 Eat a good breakfast, even if it's only a bowl of cereal. It will lift your energy levels.

8 Avoid aspirin or ibuprofen; it will only irritate your stomach further.

9 Step away from the sugar. You might be craving it but it will only add to your already unbalanced blood sugar levels. Instead, reach for a piece of fresh fruit.

10 Stomach still playing up? Try an antacid, such as my favourite citrate de bétaine, available in a French pharmacy near you. A popular antacid brand is Gaviscon.

Know your units

Unit guidelines are now the SAME for men and women. Both are advised not to regularly drink more than 14 units a week. And don't save up your units – it's best to spread them evenly across the week. If you want to cut down your drinking, have several drink-free days each week.

This is what 14 units look like:
6 pints of 4% beer
6 x 175ml glasses of 13% wine
14 x 25ml glasses of 40% spirits

For more information, visit:
drinkaware.co.uk.

The first thing you'll notice as you read on is that there's something missing from this book – quite a lot missing, actually. Important wine regions from major wine-producing countries have not been included. You won't see Champagne covered in this chapter, for instance, or Burgundy. But there's a reason for that, which I outlined in my introduction (in case you skipped it) – I'm following the coast.

France, like a lot of traditional wine-producing countries, isn't very good at shouting about other regions, even within its own country. Can you get an interesting Rhône Villages in a wine shop in the Loire? Probably not. You have to admire their parochial ways – the French in particular are passionate about their local produce and things aren't going to change any time soon. It encourages you to explore, and get to know a place better through its cuisine, from meat and fish to cheeses and pastries – and its wines, of course.

The best wines you'll find in the average wine shop in a harbour town anywhere on the Atlantic coast are most probably the ones from that region, or the neighbouring region. There are the big supermarkets, of course, which will boast huge displays, but they might not be within easy reach of the boater, or be the most exciting choice.

Local bars and restaurants also tend to favour local produce, so the following chapters are an attempt to help you choose wisely. I hold my hands up to some brazen favouritism, singling out certain regions over others. But the wine world is big, and this book is small, so I had to start somewhere – and why not with some of my favourites?

Atlantic

England, South Coast

English wine

Drive down the M20 and you would be forgiven for thinking you were in the Champagne region. But this is the Kent Downs, where row upon row of vines shimmer in the summer breeze, grapes ripening steadily. It's the same story in neighbouring Sussex, where vast swathes of the countryside are now covered in vines.

The UK has come a long way fast since its first commercial vineyard was planted in Hampshire in 1952. There are many more English vineyards now, tucked away on south-facing slopes in hidden valleys behind wind-protecting ridges of trees, where cattle once roamed and wheat fields flourished. They are award-winning vineyards, too, bringing global attention to English wine, which is now coveted by sommeliers and collectors from Tokyo to New York.

And it is sparkling wine that leads the way. Like Champagne, English sparkling wine loves chalky soils. Chalk has a visceral effect on the wine, and there's chalk in abundance in the south of England – cue the flurry of planting here in the last few years. Sparkling wine is made by some 200 UK producers – the best-known is the Nyetimber wine estate in Sussex, but other highlights include Rathfinny, Ridgeview and Wiston Estate, with which the Queen launched the new cruise ship *Britannia* in 2015. Indeed, the classic Champagne blend of Chardonnay, Pinot Noir and Pinot Meunier now accounts for half of all plantings in the UK.

Can English sparkling wine ever be as great as Champagne? Quite possibly. All the vital statistics for ageing English wine are there – finesse, acidity and concentration of flavour. It might be several hundred years behind, but what the UK industry has achieved

THREE ENGLISH VINEYARDS TO VISIT NEAR THE SOUTH COAST

• **Rathfinny Estate** is a 10-minute drive from the coastal town of Seaford in the South Downs of Sussex. Established in 2010, its aim is to produce some of the world's best sparkling wines (rathfinnyestate.com).

• **Hambledon Vineyards** is set in an idyllic Hampshire village of the same name, just north of Portsmouth. It has been making Chardonnay for more than a decade (hambledonvineyard.co.uk).

• **Nutbourne Vineyards** in Pulborough, West Sussex, made the first English still wine to win a gold medal at The International Wine & Spirit Competition (nutbournevineyards.com).

in such a short time is astonishing. High-profile awards and trophies won by English sparkling wines in international competitions have fuelled some serious investment in land that is already producing English fizz that would make Champagne proud. Even the French are snapping up land here, with Champagne Taittinger the first to announce a vineyard venture in Kent.

Gin

So as well as popping the cork on a bottle of English fizz on board, you are probably now sloshing English gin into your tonic, such is the boom in artisanal gin in recent years. The number of UK gin brands has doubled since 2010 – though, granted, gin is an easier leap to make than winemaking. It's inextricably linked to British heritage, from Hogarth's Gin Alley to Margot and Jerry in *The Good Life*.

What is gin, exactly? First alcohol is distilled from something – in the case of most high-end gins it is a grain, such as wheat. But it's the next distillation that makes good gin what it is. Cue the botanicals, which vary widely from coriander and cardamom to citrus peel and cinnamon and, of course, juniper. The only rule is that the finished gin must taste predominantly of juniper.

There are four main styles of gin – Dutch Genever, Old Tom, Compound Gin and London Dry. London Dry is what most people in the UK think of as gin – but just to confuse matters, London Dry does not have to be made in London.

What to choose? It's a matter of taste. Of the big brands, Plymouth Gin, Tanqueray No. Ten, Hendrick's and Martin Miller's are enduring favourites, but there are many artisanal gins out there to try, among them Sipsmith, Chilgrove and Williams Chase.

All at sea with Pink Gin

Thousands of barrels of Plymouth Gin were once shipped to the Royal Navy annually and naval officers visiting the Venezuelan river port of Angostura took a shine to the local bitters for their purported curative properties, including the promise to quell seasickness. By adding a dash or two of Angostura bitters to the daily ration of gin, the Pink Gin was born at sea. There are several methods of making a Pink Gin - to chill or not to chill is the big question, as the tradition is to serve it at room temperature, as there was little or no ice available at sea, but warm gin is not my thing so I wait for a ready supply of ice before drinking it.

Beer

About to crack open a bottle of Bud? Think again. British beer has reinvented itself. Across the country small breweries are refreshing, reviving and reinventing beer. From worthy Czech-style pilsners and fruity golden ales to zingy India pale ales and bold export porters and imperial stouts, there's now a style out there to suit everyone.

The craft beer movement in the UK has been nothing short of a revolution. Once the greatest brewing nation on the planet, the UK lost its way a few decades ago (the 1970s were a particular low), with traditional cask ales making way for insipid, ersatz lager. The Campaign for Real Ale (CAMRA) tried its best, but only a certain sector responded. Then in 2002 the Chancellor introduced beer duty relief for small brewers and the floodgates opened. Hundreds of craft brewers have been established in the UK since then, with many more on their way.

UK brewing pioneers include Dark Star, based in Sussex, which started importing US hops; Meantime in Greenwich, which makes characterful beers for the dinner table; one of my favourites, Oakham Ales, which has been particularly inventive with Citra hops; and Scottish craft brewer BrewDog, which has done more than most to kick-start the craze for craft – including making the best non-alcoholic beer out there, called Nanny State, for any sailors who wish to abstain but still want to party.

Island drinking

The next time you're sailing around the Isle of Wight, check out its home-grown booze. The island is attracting a growing number of creative drinks producers, from award-winning microbreweries, such as Goddards and Island Brewery, to the opening of the island's first distillery, making gin, vodka and, soon, whisky. Favourites include Goddards' seasonal Mocha Stout and Wight Mermaids Gin – try it with a splosh of tonic, a chink of ice and a sprig of samphire, plucked from one of the world's best places to drop anchor for the night, Newtown Creek.

Potted shrimps

Potted shrimps is that most British of recipes, and there's no finer topping for a slice of toast. Cut it into dinky triangles and you have an appetiser par excellence – perfect with a glass of (English) bubbly or a hoppy British ale. It should always be made with the tiny brown shrimp rather than any other kind, which is a relatively sustainable British choice according to the Marine Stewardship Council, the fount of all knowledge for such things. Supermarkets now stock them, and proper fishmongers always have them stashed in their chiller cabinets. The best are those from Morecambe Bay, in the north of the country, but for those trilling along the south coast, the more widely available North Atlantic brown shrimp makes a happy alternative. And if the brown shrimp still remains elusive, then opt for crabmeat instead.

For 4

150g unsalted butter
juice of ½ lemon
good pinch of ground mace
    or nutmeg
pinch of cayenne pepper
1 tsp anchovy essence or
    Gentleman's Relish
200g peeled brown shrimps
salt and pepper

To serve:

toast
lemon wedges
½ fresh chilli, chopped
    (optional)

Method

Melt the butter in a saucepan on a low heat, add the lemon juice, mace, cayenne pepper and anchovy essence, and simmer gently for 2 minutes to infuse the spices. Remove from the heat and cool the mixture until it is just warm. Add the shrimps and stir well. Season. Put the mixture in the fridge and stir every now and again. When the butter starts to set, fill four ramekins (I use metal ones on board) with the mixture and return to the fridge, covered with cling film. If you're chilling these in a cool box rather than a fridge, they are ready to eat. If they come straight out of the fridge, leave to soften up a little bit so the butter isn't too hard to spread on the toast. Serve with lemon wedges.

Scotland

Scotch. The name says it all, doesn't it? And you can't call it that unless it has been produced in a distillery in Scotland, and matured in Scotland. It *is* Scotland. It's responsible for a lot of the best (and a few worst) moments for sailors, and it continues to set the benchmark for whisky worldwide.

And did you know that we have a vine louse to thank for its success – in part, anyway. When phylloxera started munching its way through European vineyards in the late 1800s, customers were forced to search elsewhere for their daily tipple, so they started to look closer to home. Yes, whisky. Or I should say blended whisky. Malt whisky had to wait until the 1960s to find its market.

Blended? Malt? A **single malt** whisky is distilled at an individual distillery and produced only from malted barley. When put in the bottle, it may contain whisky from several years' production. The age on the bottle reflects the length of time the youngest whisky in that particular bottling has spent in cask. A **vatted malt** is a blend of various malt whiskies from several distilleries from a particular region, labelled Pure Malt or Scotch Malt Whisky. **Grain whisky** is produced using a continuous distillation method, maturing more quickly, with a higher strength. Single grain whiskies come from one grain distillery. **Blended whisky** is a combination of both single malts and grain whisky and accounts for the vast majority of Scotch sales.

WHISKY TOUR

No visit to Scotland would be complete without a few sips and a spin around a Scottish distillery. For sailors, Tobermory Distillery wins on the location front – situated at the edge of the town's historic multi-hued harbour, where it makes a gentle, affable ten-year-old single malt. Sailors should also make tracks, via a short taxi ride from Brodick, to the Arran Distillery on the Isle of Arran, the largest island in the Firth of Clyde. The view alone, complete with golden eagles, will make your jaw drop. While Ardbeg on the Isle of Islay shouldn't be missed – just a 15-minute cab ride from the main hub, Port Ellen. And while you're there you should visit the equally esteemed distilleries of Laphroaig and Lagavulin, both nearby.

Holland

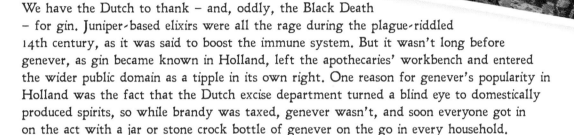

Genever

We have the Dutch to thank – and, oddly, the Black Death – for gin. Juniper-based elixirs were all the rage during the plague-riddled 14th century, as it was said to boost the immune system. But it wasn't long before genever, as gin became known in Holland, left the apothecaries' workbench and entered the wider public domain as a tipple in its own right. One reason for genever's popularity in Holland was the fact that the Dutch excise department turned a blind eye to domestically produced spirits, so while brandy was taxed, genever wasn't, and soon everyone got in on the act with a jar or stone crock bottle of genever on the go in every household.

Amsterdam is the best place to head for a tour of genever distilleries. There you'll find folk with their hands behind their backs, leaning over the bar to take their first sip from filled-to-the-rim glasses (it's a Dutch thing). Try Wynand Fockink (Pijlsteeg 31, wynand-fockink.nl), which has over 60 different kinds of genever behind the bar.

Genever is not just gin as we know it, there are different kinds. There's Oude – old, straw-coloured, with a pungent sweetness; Jonge, a newer style, which is cleaner and more delicate; and Korenwijn, which is cask-aged, with a high percentage of malted spirit.

If you find yourself moored up in Rotterdam, then head to the National Jenever Museum in Schiedam (jenevermuseum.nl) for more information on the production process. Brands to look out for include Bols, Bokma, de Kuyper and Notaris.

Beer

If genever is Holland's national tipple, then beer follows closely behind. In fact, Dutch beer easily surpasses genever in terms of volume of sales; the Dutch are the biggest exporter of beer in the world, thanks to a brand you might have heard of – Heineken. The country's long brewing tradition dates back to the 14th century, when every Dutch town boasted a brewery. By the 17th century there were 700 breweries in Holland. There aren't so many these days, of course – the market is dominated by a handful of big brands, namely Heineken, Amstel and Grolsch. But there are a growing number of craft brewers dotted throughout the country to look out for.

Channel Islands

On a good day, in the middle of summer, it looks a bit like the Caribbean. White sandy beaches, turquoise waters, the odd palm blowing in the breeze, the occasional subtropical flower showing off garish colours. Welcome to the Channel Islands – a dependent territory of the English Crown, situated 10 to 30 miles off the north-west coast of France. Just to be clear, they are not part of the UK – Guernsey and Jersey are self-governing nations with their own parliaments, and while they are not members of the European Union, they do have a special trade relationship. The surrounding islets of Alderney, Sark, Herm, Jethou and Lihou are part of Guernsey's jurisdiction.

Jersey is the largest of the Channel Islands, sitting 14 miles west of the Cherbourg peninsula and 38 miles south-east of Guernsey. We're talking 9 miles from east to west, 5 miles from north to south, and 45 miles of coastline, with oysters, lobsters, Jersey Royal potatoes and dairy products made from the milk of prize Jersey cows the star produce here.

Jersey has always felt a strong affinity with France, and many Jersey families can trace their ancestry back to France. Indeed, most road names are written in French, so it's no surprise that this relationship stretches to wine, too. The Loire, Champagne and Bordeaux top the list of most popular purchases, thanks to islanders making frequent trips to the country, but Jersey makes its own booze, too – from wine and beer to cider and even gin.

Beer

Beer has been brewed in Jersey for centuries but the first commercial brewery opened in Ann Street in Jersey's capital, St Helier, in 1871. And it still makes beer today, trading as The Liberation Group – a reference to the German occupation during the Second World War. The island was liberated on 9 May 1945 and on that date every year Jersey has a 'national' holiday, when they drink copious amounts of the brewery's flagship cask ale, Liberation Ale.

Cider

But before beer, there was cider. The first recorded evidence of cider production in Jersey dates from the 15th century and by the 17th century apple was the island's national crop, long before the famous Jersey Royal potato. Production dropped dramatically from the 1850s onwards but a small number of cider producers remain on the island, including La Robeline Cider Company. Try the Cidre dé Jèrri, available in shops around the island or from the company's own mobile bar, a familiar sight at markets, fairs and fêtes.

Other Channel Islands' booze to try

Another cider producer is La Mare Wine Estate, which, as the name suggests, also produces wine. This working vineyard and distillery can be found in a quiet corner in the northern part of the island. The estate has nine acres of vineyards producing 20,000 bottles of sparkling, white and red wines a year, thanks to Jersey's mild climate. La Mare also produces a VSOP Jersey apple brandy, plus gin and vodka.

Guernsey also produces its own gin – Wheadon's – at the Bella Luce Hotel & Restaurant in St Martins, where there are gin tastings and masterclasses, while Randalls Brewery has been turning out beer on Guernsey since 1868. There's cider here, too – Rocquette waves the flag for the island's cider heritage. Even sister island Sark has got in on the action, with 27 acres of newly planted vineyards.

France, West Coast

Calvados

Of all Normandy's produce, it's the apple brandy that excites me the most. Calvados is much misunderstood in the UK, or worse, ignored. The good stuff is delicious, multi-layered and mouth-watering, with dazzling complexity – a must for every boat stash.

The large négociant houses predictably dominate but the real delights come from the smaller artisan producers who distil from their own orchards, such as Christian Drouin.

Drouin is in the Pays d'Auge, the oldest Calvados appellation, established in 1942. It was created to protect it, to stop the French military from nicking it all, or so the story goes. And it was at Drouin that I got to taste something very special – a 1939 Calvados. It was hidden from the Germans during the Second World War in a hole in the ground. It is surprisingly fruity, with a peppery hit – and still very much alive and kicking.

These days there are around 300 Calvados producers in Normandy, but once every farmer made it, along with cider, selling their distillations to larger producers for blending, some bottling their own.

Cider

And talking of cider, Normandy makes some of the best. It has a dryness and a lip-smacking acidity that you don't often find in British counterparts, and an affinity with a vast range of foods. The best place to drink Normandy cider? Honfleur harbour. It's no surprise that the Impressionist painters used to flock here in their droves – the place is magical. Wander the tangle of cobbled streets, stocking up on cheese for the galley from one of the smart delis, before settling at one of the harbourside bars, such as Le Perroquet Vert, one of our favourites.

Cider route

For the full experience, hire a car for a day or two and follow a cider route, visiting producers and stocking up for your journey. Go to calvados-tourisme.co.uk – it has a route already mapped out, complete with opening times and contact details. The circular route highlights 20 Calvados and cider producers covering some of the best bits of the Pays d'Auge, taking you through half-timbered medieval villages, such as the Parisian's favourite, Beuvron-en-Auge, past lush meadows full of happy cows and orchards as far as the eye can see.

Wine and spirits

The Loire is the largest wine-growing region for white wine in France, the second largest region for AOC rosé wines, and the third largest region for AOC wines. Only Champagne produces more sparkling wines. No area can match the Loire's range of dry, sweet and sparkling wines, made using grapes such as Cabernet Franc, Melon de Bourgogne, Gamay, Pineau d'Aunis, Sauvignon Blanc and Chenin Blanc, with styles ranging from light, crisp Muscadets to raspberry-rich Chinons.

Here's a heads-up – no other area in France sells fine old whites at these kinds of prices. Key Loire names to watch out for include Didier Dagueneau in Pouilly (pricey), Domaine de la Butte in Bourgueil, Domaine Huet in Vouvray, and Thierry Germain in Saumur.

It could take you months to work your way along the Loire river's 1,000km length, with its 7,000 wine estates cultivating 70,000 hectares (nearly 173,000 acres) of vines – though many sailors will doubtless not venture beyond Muscadet at the river's mouth, which is currently having a bit of a moment (buy those with 'Sur Lie' on the label).

But I'm going to bang the drum for Vouvray, further up the river, and neighbouring Montlouis-sur-Loire.

Vouvray produces white wines made of Chenin Blanc, with a considerable lifespan – ten years or more. This remarkably diverse grape has inspired winemakers the world over, but nowhere does it scale such heights as in Vouvray. It does dry, medium, sparkling and sweet whites, aged in cellars dug deep into the limestone hills.

It's not all about the whites, either. Loire reds can be equally delicious, with Saumur-Champigny at the top of my list. Relatively low in alcohol and high in acidity, they are supple yet sparky, with great fruit intensity – and delicious quaffed slightly chilled.

Travel further down the west coast of France and you'll hit the Charentes region. This is where the most elegant of all brandies is made, in the chalkiest soils, around the little town of Cognac. All Cognac must be distilled twice in pot stills, and aged for not less than two years in oak.

But Cognac labels can be confusing. While some companies have their own ways of categorising their brandies, there are three most common categories, ranked by age, expense and (usually) quality – VS (a minimum of two years' ageing), VSOP (four years' ageing) and XO (Extra Old – six or more years' ageing). With VS, no one will blink if you splash a mixer into it. But by the time you get up to XO, we're talking huge price tags, and drinking it neat.

Which brings us neatly to Bordeaux. There has been an alarming increase in recent years in the prices paid for the most famous names here, thanks to new markets opening up, such as China. Though Bordeaux has always been seen as a status symbol – it's the biggest producer of fine wines in the world. But don't let that scare you off – in a good year there are decent wines to be had in the more basic appellations and lower classifications. In a bad year, not so much. Basic red Bordeaux can look mighty thin next to its consistently ripe Cabernet equivalent from the New World. On the bottom rung are Bordeaux Rouge and Bordeaux Blanc, with Bordeaux Supérieur subject to slightly more rigorous regulations.

Then there are the large prestigious areas within the Bordeaux region to explore, like the Médoc and the Graves, Pessac-Léognan and St-Émilion, each with its own AC, pecking order and exciting line-up of wines, plus smaller but no less important regions, such as Pomerol, with its elegant, timeless reds. For better value for money, check out the wines from the appellations of Blaye and Bourg.

Bordeaux has numerous classifications, too. In 1855, the leading châteaux of the Médoc were classified into five levels by Bordeaux's wine brokers, identifying the soils with the highest potential – fifth growths through to the top level first growths in ascending order of quality – plus a Graves property, Haut-Brion. Below this is Crus Bourgeois, which has its own pecking order.

So which area to look at on this coast after the bling of Bordeaux? Well, if you're me, then Irouléguy. I love this tiny appellation, which makes the country's only Basque wine. Fresh rosés, savoury, balanced reds and aromatic whites made with largely indigenous grapes that are quite rare, grown on south-facing terraces high above the Atlantic.

Artichoke, feta and ham tart

This recipe combines two of my favourite ingredients, artichokes and air-dried ham. Artichokes are Brittany's other claim to fame, after its sparkling seafood. From the sea, Brittany is a land of rocky coves on a sharply indented coastline, eroded granite and sandstone cliffs tumbling into rough seas and headlands that stretch out into the water. But behind the rugged shores you'll find fields of artichokes, which grow especially well on the salty land. Combine that with cheese and ham in a tart and you've got one smart boat nibble. And as we're sailing down towards the south-west coast of France, you could make that Bayonne ham, a speciality of the region and a key ingredient in Basque cuisine. The espelette pepper rubbed into the skin gives the ham a unique tanginess. Though Parma or Serrano ham will work just as well here.

For 4

320g ready-made puff
    pastry sheet
200g feta cheese
100ml crème fraîche
390g (240g drained) tin of
    artichoke hearts, drained
    and sliced into quarters
4 air-dried ham slices, torn
pinch of dried oregano
salt and pepper

Method

Preheat the oven to 200°C/fan 180°C/gas 6 and line a baking sheet with greaseproof paper, and then the puff pastry sheet. In a bowl, smash up the feta with a fork then stir in the cream to make a paste. Season to taste. Spread the feta mixture evenly over the pastry. Arrange the quartered artichoke hearts on top, scrunch the torn ham onto the base and sprinkle with oregano. Cook for 10 minutes, then reduce the heat to 180°C/fan 160°C/gas 4 and cook for a further 15 minutes, or until golden brown. Serve warm, or at room temperature, cut into slices.

Spain, North and West Coast

Spain has come a long way fast. What has happened in the wine industry here in the last 20 years has been nothing short of a revolution. Along with Italy, Spain is a great wine nation of the Mediterranean. But before we head south, there's some Atlantic-influenced vineyard action that's not to be missed.

One of the joys of travelling is trying local produce – and it doesn't get more local than the piercing, appley whites of the Basque country. I'm talking Txakoli – (pronounced chack-oh-lee), a farmhouse white that dates back to 1520 and is still served in the Bay of Biscay cities, poured from a great height (it's a flavour thing, they'll tell you), a perfect accompaniment to the region's famous *pintxos*, the Basque equivalent of tapas.

In neighbouring Asturias, they might not have a tradition of winemaking but they do have spectacular cider, and a visit to this part of Spain is not

complete without a night out at a *sidreria*, where, like Txakoli, the cider is also poured from a great height to accentuate the flavours.

Galicia is known as the region of a thousand rivers. The coast is peppered with bays and inlets, known locally as 'rías'. Every ría is fed by at least one estuary and it's the meeting of the fresh and salt waters that many claim results in the enviable quality of Galicia's seafood.

Rías Baixas (pronounced ree-ass by-shuss) is Galicia's most famous wine region. With vines trained on distinctive granite pergolas that hover well above shoulder height, the wine region owes its living to the sea. The whites – and it is mostly whites here – have an attractive salinity, and when combined with sought-after minerality, thanks to the limestone and chalky soils, you have the perfect partner for the region's abundant seafood.

The key grape here is Albariño. Why? Because its thick skin resists the mildew that is a constant threat. There is increasing experimentation with the grape, too – using oak and even ageing the wines. Labels to check out include Pazo Señorans and Martín Códax.

Also try Godello, the region's other star grape. Some of the best come from the Valdeorras wine region, from producers such as Rafael Palacios. In good years Galicia is building a reputation for its reds, made from grapes such as Mencía, which shines in neighbouring Bierzo.

Portugal

On the Atlantic fringe of Europe, Portugal has been quietly getting on with making its individual wines, and making quite a name for itself in the process. While other countries were busy planting French varieties, Portugal stuck to her guns with the country's indigenous grapes, with names such as Amor-não-me-Deixes (which translates as 'love don't leave me') and Borrado das Moscas ('fly droppings'), which is turning out wines that excite, from producers such as Luís Pato and Dirk Niepoort.

Port

Inland from Porto, steeped in tradition, they still tread grapes by foot in ancient stone *lagares*. It's a taste of a place where time has stopped. I'm talking, of course, about Portugal's most famous wine, port, which is made in the northern region of the Douro. Here, ripe, thick-skinned red grapes such as Touriga Nacional are turned into extraordinary deep, sweet, strong wines, made in many different styles. There are two basic categories: those aged in bottle and those aged in wood. And within these two categories, there are many different styles of port.

Vintage port, for example, starts out as it would for dry table wine. But then, when there is still a good amount of unfermented sugar left, spirit is added to stop fermentation. The alcohol shoots up and the wine becomes sweet. It's put into oak for a year or so, then bottled, and left for at least ten years before drinking.

Aged tawny port, on the other hand, is aged before bottling. It's left in barrels for six or more years to turn tawny in colour, and then it's blended with different vintages for added complexity before bottling.

Other port styles include ruby port, named for its distinct ruby colour, young, approachable and fruity; reserve ruby port (aged a bit longer), sometimes known as vintage character; late bottled vintage (made from a single year's harvest); and white port, glorious sipped on a warm day on board, served as a long drink with ice, a slice of orange, a good splash of tonic and a sprig of mint.

While you're in Porto, a visit to the port lodges is a must. Located in the heart of the historic area of Vila Nova de Gaia, just across the river from the old city centre, you'll find venerable producers such as Taylor's (taylor.pt). You can tour the cellars with its extensive reserves of wood-aged and vintage port, before hitting the Library Bar for a tasting, or the stunning terrace on a sunny day.

Madeira

And while we're on the subject of Portuguese fortified wines, one mustn't forget Madeira. The Atlantic island, 750 miles south-east of Lisbon, produces some of the most exciting fortified wines in the world. Grapes growing on the island's terraced volcanic slopes ripen in the humid, subtropical climate to produce a variety of styles of wine denoted by their natural sugar content. They range from Sercial grapes, producing the driest styles, through to Malvasia grapes, which make the sweetest styles.

Wine

And last but definitely not least are those table wines. Since Portugal's entry into the European Economic Community in 1986, things have changed dramatically here on the table-wine front. Some of Europe's most underrated dry red and white table wines now come from Portugal, made from grape varieties rarely found elsewhere.

There's the Minho, in the far north-west, just below the Spanish border, where rolling green hills rammed with orchards and vines turn out Vinho Verde with a much improved flavour intensity. The Douro, while famous for port, is also a source of top dry red table wines with a structure, power and juiciness that will have you running back for more. Dão is another exciting region, 30 miles south of the Douro river, along with Bairrada to the west, not far from the Atlantic, where juicy, acidic Baga has to make up half the blend of any red, and where the region's speciality, roast suckling pig, is best downed with its sparkling reds. Finally, there's the Alentejo, the biggest wine region in Portugal, covering virtually the entire south-east, stretching across hot, dry, rolling plains, where grapes produce plummy, peppery reds and surprisingly refreshing whites.

Sardine-stuffed eggs

This is Portugal's answer to tapas, and a mainstay of the Portuguese restaurant (and my mum's) buffet since the 1970s. It's also rather handy for the boat, and best quaffed with a cold beer. Ok, so it's probably not the most sophisticated example of Portuguese cuisine – the country has a rich culinary legacy that can be traced right back to medieval times. Portugal's maritime past and its fertile coastline led to a cuisine rich in seafood, while its colonies in Africa, Asia and the New World also left their culinary mark. I love Portuguese cuisine because it's refreshingly simple and uses straightforward ingredients, and this recipe is a good example. My favourites are the soups and stews, and the pastries are legendary – *pastéis de nata* (custard tart) is one of my all-time favourites, and I've made many a trip to Lisboa Patisserie on London's Golborne Road to get my fix.

For 4

4 large free-range eggs, hard-boiled
   and peeled
1 tin sardine fillets in olive oil, drained
2 tbsp mayonnaise
juice of ½ lemon
2 tsp Dijon mustard

To serve:

4 pitted black olives, chopped
1 tbsp capers, chopped
handful of flat-leaf parsley,
   finely chopped
grated zest of 1 lemon

Method

Slice the eggs in half lengthways. Scoop out the yolks, leaving the whites intact, and place in a bowl. Add the remaining ingredients and mash with a fork to a chunky paste. As you're on the water, you could cut a small slice off the bottom of each egg so that they don't slide off the plate – your call. Refill the eggs with the prepared paste and top each one with chopped black olives and capers, with the parsley and lemon scattered over the top.

Canaries

Canary Island wines were once famous in the UK. Ok, so we're talking 16th and 17th centuries here, but back then we couldn't get enough of them. And now it seems our attention is back on the wines, which boast a tang and vibrancy that would make any good winemaker proud.

There are ten different appellations in the Canary Islands – one for each island, except Tenerife, which has been divided into five more. But you won't find much Chardonnay and Cabernet here. Instead, the choice of vines harks back to the history and geography of islands that were once important staging posts on maritime trading routes.

The main grape variety when the Canaries were major wine exporters was Malvasia, and this is still the main grape grown in La Palma and on Lanzarote. The other principal variety is Listán Blanco, and this is supplemented by a wide range of other grapes. The principal red grape is Listán Negro.

The Canaries' USP is the volcanic soil – and nowhere is this more dramatic than on Lanzarote. Called the 'Island of Fire', it suffered devastating volcanic eruptions over six years from 1730. Much of the middle of the island is a sea of petrified black lava. But the resourceful Lanzaroteños developed a way of growing the vines that is completely unique to them, albeit rather labour intensive. Situated entirely on the black volcanic slopes and covering just 20 square miles, La Geria wine region produces most of the island's wine, and is home to the majority of the island's 18 *bodegas*.

There are more than 10,000 funnel-shaped hollows, called *zocos*, which each contain one vine. They are filled with soil and covered with a thick porous mulch, made from volcanic granules, which feeds the plants and absorbs moisture from the night air. To protect the vines from the constant winds, a horseshoe-shaped wall of lava rock surrounds each hollow – which is quite a spectacle.

White wines rule here. The Malvasia grape accounts for some 75 per cent of production, some of it used to make the sublime honey-coloured sweet wines that made the island famous back in the 1500s, while the rest is used to make dry whites – the best showing off seductive fruit with a sought-after minerality.

The wine is a perfect match for the abundant grilled fish, which is eaten with the national dish of *papas arrugadas*, literally 'wrinkled potatoes' (small unpeeled potatoes boiled in sea water until it has virtually evaporated), and *mojo rojo* (an addictive sweet red pepper sauce) and *mojo verde* (a coriander or parsley green sauce).

US, East Coast

Wine

New York State makes more wine than any other state in the USA, except for California, which makes more than 12 times that. Surprising, huh? In the last few decades it has been busy establishing itself as a serious wine region, with some 320 producers at the last count.

The most vineyard action can be seen in boaters' favourite the Finger Lakes region, which now has over 100 wineries. Long Island boasts more than 50 producers, which is not bad considering it's only been making wine for just over three decades, while the Hudson River region has more than 30 producers.

Finger Lakes does a nice line in reasonably priced Rieslings – always good chilled on board – from producers such as Hermann J Wiemer, Fox Run and Dr Frank. And while Riesling is undoubtedly the star, other grape varieties to watch here include Grüner Veltliner, Cabernet Franc, Blaufränkisch and Gewürztraminer.

Further south, Maryland wants a slice of the quality wine action. Rarely available outside the state, the wines are made in five different microclimates, from the more humid inland areas to the cooler, drier area next to Chesapeake Bay. And anything goes here, from Italian Sangiovese to hybrids such as Seyval Blanc, as winemakers continue to experiment.

But it's neighbouring Virginia that is getting wine buffs in a tizz. The crusade to put Virginia on the wine map stretches back to Thomas Jefferson. Aspiring winemakers have been planting classic European varieties in this lush, humid horse country for years in an effort to make decent wine, yet it's only in the last decade or so that their efforts have been rewarded. Virginia now has a total of seven American Viticultural Areas (AVAs) and a growing following for its wines.

Craft beer

And if you're not enjoying a glass of wine on the US East Coast, then you're enjoying a cold glass of craft beer. A one-trick corporate pony not so long ago, awash with the insipid likes of Budweiser, Miller and Coors, there has been an explosion in the USA of independently run microbreweries producing lovingly crafted, strong, pungent, flavour-packed ales. Add to that hipster credibility, with hot new bars around the world offering a line-up of US craft beers, and you have nothing short of a brewing revolution.

The East Coast has more than its fair share of forward-thinking breweries. Names to look out for include Brooklyn Brewery in New York, Tree House Brewing in Monson, Massachusetts, New England Brewing in Woodbridge, Connecticut, and the Maine Beer Company in Freeport, Maine. In Boston, you can take your pick from larger outfits, such as Samuel Adams, to smaller operations, such as Idle Hands and Mystic.

Florida Keys

The Gulf of Mexico shimmers on one side, while the Atlantic pounds on the other – this is as far south as you can go in the United States. Sometimes called America's Caribbean (it's nearer to Cuba than Miami), the Florida Keys offer an end-of-the-road remoteness and a languid tropicality that has attracted fishermen, sailors, divers, drinkers and misfits of all shapes and sizes, among them Truman Capote, Jimmy Buffett and Ernest Hemingway. It's Hemingway's time spent here that is responsible for a lot of the mythology surrounding the 800-plus islands that make up the Keys – one where anything goes and everyone parties, with Key West at the end of that road.

But for a real flavour of the Keys, head to

Stock Island, a working waterfront community – one of the few left in the USA, a few minutes' drive from Key West proper. Head to the quayside, to the Hogfish Bar and Grill, for perfect conch fritters washed down with a cocktail called Rum Runner.

Rum-running was a widespread and honourable profession in the Florida Keys during Prohibition, immortalised in Hemingway's novel, *To Have and Have Not*. Rum is legal these days, of course, and it's consumed in vast quantities here – most notably in a Rum Runner, a frozen pastel-coloured drink made with three types of rum and an assortment of fruit liqueurs.

The elegant, immaculately restored 19th-century clapboard houses that line the streets of Key West are a constant echo of the past, with their plaques declaring that wreckers once owned them. Ships regularly went aground on the shallow coral reef and the enterprising locals made a substantial living from salvaging those wrecks.

The last mile of U.S. Route 1 takes you down Whitehead Street – and straight into the Green Parrot Bar. Here you can try the locals' favourite, Mother's Milk – rum, soda, and a splash of cola – as you shoot the breeze with anyone who'll listen. Whitehead Street is also where Hemingway once lived, so if you want to continue in his footsteps, head to Sloppy Joe's bar. It's named after Joe Russell, who ran a speakeasy in Prohibition-hit America, stocking it with booze he transported illegally from Cuba. He was the inspiration for one of Hemingway's larger than life characters, Harry Morgan, in *To Have and Have Not*.

Found a coconut? Then try a Saoco (sa-oh-ko). Traditionally made with the water of a green coconut, you can also make this with a ripe (hard brown) coconut. To open the latter, punch in the 'eyes' (round dots on the top of the shell) with a screwdriver, and then drain the coconut over a glass. Combine with a splash of rum, a squeeze of fresh lime and a teaspoon of sugar, and pour over ice.

For something non-alcoholic, try *batidos* – Florida's answer to a milkshake, served at juice bars and *loncherías* (Cuban snack bars) throughout the state. The main ingredient is fresh fruit, not dairy, with ice to chill. *Batidos* are made with everything from pineapples and strawberries to more exotic fruits such as atemoya and mamey, brilliant thirst-quenchers on a hot day.

Black bean salsa

The Caribbean meets Florida in this lively boat bar snack, best scooped up with a pile of tortilla chips. The Sunshine State has everything a boat cook could want: the Atlantic Ocean and Gulf of Mexico supply sweet stone crabs, spiny lobsters, Gulf shrimp, oysters and more than 500 different varieties of finfish. Not forgetting the nation's largest freshwater swamp, the Everglades, which offers bounty for the more adventurous cook, with palm hearts and frogs' legs – even alligator (the tail and jaw meat is considered the most desirable). But I'm keeping it real, and veggie, with this spicy, filling salsa, which doubles up as a colourful side for grilled fish.

For 4

1 x 230g tin black beans, rinsed and drained
1 x 160g tin sweetcorn, drained
1 ripe avocado, finely chopped
1 red pepper, finely chopped
2 spring onions, trimmed and finely sliced
1 tbsp finely chopped jalapeno chillies (or to taste)
handful of coriander or mint leaves, chopped
1 tsp ground cumin
2 tbsp extra virgin olive oil
1 lime or lemon
salt and pepper

To serve:

tortilla chips

Method

In a bowl, combine the beans, sweetcorn, avocado, red pepper, onions, jalapenos and coriander. Add the cumin, drizzle with oil, squeeze over the lime or lemon juice and season to taste. Serve with a big pile of tortilla chips.

South Africa

As wine country goes, it doesn't get much more beautiful than this. Get past the Cape's jagged, mauve, mountain-fringed coastline and you've got verdant valleys galore. Add to that the graceful Cape Dutch gables, some serious cooking, and even classier wines and you have the essential ingredients for the perfect break from the high seas.

And haven't things changed fast? It's only been exporting wine for little more than a couple of decades, since the fall of apartheid heralded the lifting of sanctions, and the country is now the world's ninth largest wine producer, with a new generation of wine estates. From their modest beginnings in the Dutch East India Company's gardens below Table Mountain, South Africa's vineyards now spread over 100,000 hectares. There are many different wine regions, and new wineries going up all the time – many backed by foreign investors.

This new breed of winemaker has familiarised itself with the rest of the vinous globe and is more open to criticism, producing some revolutionary wines with a true South African identity, combining Old World philosophies with New World techniques. Chenin Blanc is still king in South Africa, followed by the other top four grape varieties – Cabernet Sauvignon, Colombard, Shiraz and Sauvignon Blanc.

The Cape area produces most of the country's wines, in coastal districts such as Durbanville and Constantia, and inland areas such as Robertson and Worcester, with Paarl and Stellenbosch the main wine districts.

Cooled in the summer by sea breezes, Constantia is the nearest wine region to Cape Town. With its gated communities and imposing villas, it's really a suburb of the city, a 20-minute drive from the centre, on the eastern flank of the Cape Peninsula. White wines are the name of the game here, particularly Sauvignon Blanc and Sémillon.

The drive from Cape Town to Franschhoek is also a must. The valley is jaw-droppingly beautiful, the town impossibly pretty, with its well-kept veranda-wrapped homes, pastel-painted boutiques and chic restaurants, with Le Quartier Français at its well-coiffured epicentre. Wine highlights – and there are many – include Chamonix, Warwick Estate (where you can book a picnic and sit under the trees scoffing their biltong and sun-dried tomato pâté, while working your way through some top-notch wines), and Raats Family Wines.

But I have a particular passion for Swartland, where the landscape changes from verdant valley to sun-drenched savannah. To make the best of your visit, stay the night in the funky little town of Riebeek Kasteel, with its laid-back cafés and sleepy streets. Wine highlights include those from Mullineux, Kloovenburg, Scali, Badenhorst and Sadie, showing a purity of fruit and an elegant minerality.

There are other up-and-coming and established vineyard areas in South Africa, sure – which is why there is such excitement surrounding the country's wine industry. For more information, visit winesofsa.co.uk.

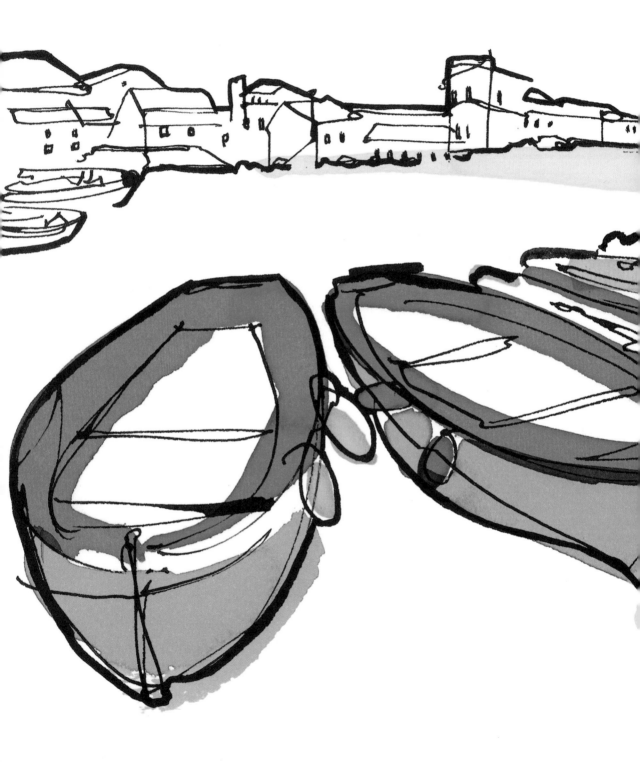

Med

Who doesn't love the Med?

Colours fading into pastel tints in the translucent light; whitewashed villas tumbling down hillsides; the warm smell of pine drifting on the breeze; chattering cicadas, fragrant markets; languorous squares, bustling ports.

Bordered by Europe in the north, Asia in the east, and Africa in the south, the Med is 969,100 square miles of deep-blue sea – 'drunk with joy under an azure sky', as one of my all-time favourite food writers, Claudia Roden, puts it.

Western civilisation can be traced right back here. The Med has been overrun by different cultures over the centuries, indelibly linked to its food and drink – which is why we have such an affinity with it. We understand that much of our language and most of our culture comes from the Med, and we are especially drawn to its cuisine. The Mediterranean table is all about sparseness and making do, using a small number of ingredients. There's a respect for ingredients, a simplicity of flavour and a level of quality that says it all, with wines that are sought after, and emulated, all over the globe.

Produce has a sense of place that imbues the character of each region – a particularly intense black olive, say, or a difficult-to-pronounce grape variety that you won't find anywhere else, and mountain-herb-laced spirits that both settle the stomach and make the party swing in a way that never quite works back home – I know, I tried.

France, South Coast

It's not hard to see why tourists flock to Provence. It's extraordinarily beautiful, from the crystal-clear water inlets to rugged mountain massifs, interspersed with fat-cattle-dotted plateaux, lush valleys and jaw-dropping ravines. But to truly understand Provence, you need to hire a car and explore inland, among fields of lavender, rosemary-scented *garrigues* and well-tended rows of vines.

We can't get enough of its delicate rosé. Provence is France's number one AOC rosé wine-producing region, accounting for nearly 40 per cent of all French rosé, so pink rules around here. And Provence rosé is a tad different to the rest. Provence has gone for a paler shade of pink (it's the way they make it, often blending in local variety Rolle, aka Vermentino). And yes, the shade really does matter, they will tell you.

Of course, it's not all about pink. There are some seriously interesting reds being made all over Provence and some jolly whites, such as the herbal wines of Cassis, made around the small port to the east of Marseille, that is perfect for bouillabaisse, and Bellet with its aromatic Rolle. Bandol, too, makes wines to excite, mainly reds made from Mourvèdre, often blended with Grenache and Cinsault.

Provence wine trail

The Route des Vins de Provence connects 350 wine
producers, from Nice to the Camargue, steering you easily,
via distinctive signage, from one cellar to another through
picturesque towns and along scenic country lanes. Start your
journey with a visit to the Maison des Vins Côtes de Provence, in
Les Arcs sur Argens (www.maison-des-vins.fr) where you will get an
introduction to the terroir, wines and gastronomy of the appellation. It
features over 800 wines sold at producer prices, plus a range of regional
specialities, tasting sessions and wine appreciation classes. There's a
good restaurant on site, too, called La Vigne à Table. You want to
stay over? Château de Berne (chateauberne.com) is a smart place
to make your base. Situated near Lorgues, in AOC Côtes-de-
Provence, this vast estate has 198 acres of vines, plus a small
but perfectly formed four-star hotel, a cooking school,
a perfume school, a wine school and a watercolour
school – not to mention a posh restaurant and a
small bistro inside the on-site wine shop.

There are other iconic drinks made in Provence, too. There's anise-laced pastis, found on every shelf in town – the lynchpin of one of Hemingway's favourite cocktails when he used to hang out in this part of the country: Champagne with a splash of pastis, aka the aptly named 'Death in the Afternoon'. There are complex grape brandies known as marc, a stellar digestif. And heady fortified wines, which embrace the natural sweetness of the local Muscat grape (Muscat de Beaumes de Venise), delicious chilled on deck on a sunny afternoon and a local favourite as an aperitif.

And it's not all about Provence in the south of France. The Languedoc is France's New World, with pioneering winemakers making thrilling wines, transforming it from the plonk capital it once was. In the eastern part of the region, above Montpellier, you'll find innovative producers such as Domaine de l'Hortus in Pic Saint-Loup, and in the west, important appellations such as rugged Corbières and more polished Minervois, peppered with ambitious producers making toothsome wines. And not forgetting neighbouring Roussillon, with its natural wine enthusiasts (see page 170) and its vins doux naturels, sweet wines that make great aperitifs, from Muscat de Rivesaltes to Maury and Banyuls.

Two-olive tapenade

I could happily live on a desert island with nothing more than bread, wine and olives. This classic Provençal spread is useful to the point of essential on board. Always have a jar to hand stashed in your boat larder. It keeps for weeks under a thick layer of olive oil and can be turned into a pasta sauce, used to top potatoes, made into vinaigrette, great as an instant crust on fish fillets, or made into a sandwich. It's best, though, slathered on slices of toasted baguette and washed down with a well-chilled drink – the ultimate boat nibble.

It's brilliant with a delicate, pale pink rosé, unimpeachable with a gin and tonic and a fine accompaniment to pastis. If you have access to fresh basil, use it, but a pinch of dried thyme will suffice. It's usually blitzed in a food processor but I love this chunky version chopped finely by hand. Traditionally it's made from the small black olives so beloved in Provence, but I also like the addition of an astringent kick of green. I sometimes add 3 or 4 chopped sun-dried tomatoes when I have them, and a teaspoon of sailor's favourite rum, which adds a balancing sweetness. Avoid rubbery pitted olives in brine if you can; instead, prise out the stones with a sharp knife.

Makes 1 smallish bowl (a little goes a long way)

100g whole black olives (preferably Niçoise or Kalamata)
100g whole green olives
3 tbsp capers, well-rinsed if packed in salt
3 anchovy fillets
1 fat garlic clove, crushed
½ tsp dried thyme
½ lemon
5 tbsp extra virgin olive oil
pepper

Method

Remove the olive stones with a sharp knife. Chop, and then chop some more until you get a chunky paste. Chop the capers, anchovies and garlic and stir into the olives. Add the thyme, squeeze over the lemon juice and stir in the olive oil. Season to taste with pepper.

Corsica

Corsica is all about the mountains. The villages learned long ago to leave the coast to the invaders, who came and went, among them Greeks, Saracens and Etruscans. And Corsicans are mountain people – as the peaks rise up to 2,700m, there are places where the snow never even melts, and where tourists rarely venture. They prefer to keep as much of the island's savage, natural beauty as they can to themselves, and that includes the wine, as little is exported.

In fact, the mountains have a big role to play in the wines here. Despite Corsica being France's most southerly vineyard area, and its sunniest, it is most definitely not the hottest – thanks to those mountains, and the constant sea breezes, which whip around the island, tempering the heat and offering humidity.

It's also thanks to the mountains that the vineyard areas are all quite separate from each other, with different landscapes and soils, ranging from schist in the east to granite soils on the west and south coasts. In fact, though the vineyard area is tiny compared to the might of Bordeaux, it is split into nine different AOCs, from Coteaux du Cap Corse and Patrimonio to Ajaccio and Sartène. But if you're thinking that the island is carpeted with vines, you can think again – the mountainous terrain makes much of the island inaccessible, so the bulk of wine production takes place on the eastern coastline, between Bastia and Porto-Vecchio, where the land is flattest.

Corse Figari is the most southerly (and windy) AOC, with Coteaux du Cap Corse the furthest north, situated on an equally blowy finger of land that juts out into the sea, the soils schist rather than granite. Just below it, you'll find Patrimonio, where many of Corsica's finest wines are to be found, the vineyards tucked into folds in the hillside.

Corsica's wines have real interest, especially for those bored with the usual international varieties. Many of the wines here have a particular aromatic quality, thanks to the maquis, which gives them a moreish herbal quality. The best combine the elegance of Provence with the boldness of Tuscany, and command similarly high prices. Producers to watch out for include Saparale, Comte Abbatucci, Domaine de Torraccia and Arena.

As well as the standard southern French grapes (Grenache and Syrah), Corsica boasts its own indigenous varieties. Among them is Nielluccio, related to Sangiovese (from Tuscany), which offers rich red berries laced with spice and a whiff of violet, the basis of red wines from Patrimonio; Sciacarello is grown mainly in the granite soils of southern Corsica and comes with a peppery kick. Big among the white grapes is Vermentino – called Malvasia here, it produces a distinctive, rich, floral mouthful that works particularly well with the region's punchy cuisine.

Matching Corsican wine with food

The whites, particularly Vermentino, are fresh and zesty and go well with seafood, such as the local langouste (spiny lobsters) and sweet spider crabs. Sciacarello is perfect with the classic mountain dishes of wild boar casserole and veal stuffed with olives. Dark, intense Nielluccio, meanwhile, is happy with more earthy dishes, such as a slow-cooked game stew called tianu, and a great match for Corsica's splendid range of charcuterie, considered the best in France.

Italy

There are vines everywhere you look in Italy, from the foothills of the Alps to the tiny island of Pantelleria, off the coast. The Ancient Greeks called it the land of wine, and it's still very much that, with the world's richest variety of individual wine styles, distinctive terroirs and indigenous grape varieties.

Italy's top wines rival the best from Bordeaux – and it's not just the Tuscans and Piedmontese who are making the best stuff; there are serious reds, and even a few whites, coming out of every region. And it's all happened so fast – in just a couple of generations. Before then, the vast majority of wine was shipped in bulk or blended for export.

I'm not going to try to cover the entire country, but just give you my highlights (and obsess about one bit in particular – Etna), hopefully giving you a little bit of info that might be helpful if you are buying a bottle of wine in a harbour somewhere in Italy.

Like France, Italy is fiercely regional – you won't see many wines from Piedmont on the shelves in Puglia. In fact, to really understand Italy's wines, it is best to think of it as a group of regions, rather than a single country.

Starting in the north-west, we've got the wine buff's favourite, Piedmont. Barolo and Barbaresco are its two best wines, and named after villages here. Most of the rest of Piedmont's most famous wines are named after the grapes from which they are made: Barbera, Dolcetto, Moscato and Nebbiolo, the king of the grapes around these parts.

Tuscany, meanwhile, is Italy's wine powerhouse and the birthplace of four of the country's most important red wines: Chianti, Chianti Classico, Brunello di Montalcino and Vino Nobile di Montepulciano. Though all are made with the same grape variety, Sangiovese, the wines taste quite different, thanks to the undulating hills and valleys in Tuscany. You prefer white? Vernaccia di San Gimignano is Tuscany's most traditional white wine and dates back to the 13th century.

Off the coast of Tuscany, you'll find the Italian island of Sardinia. Sardinia makes fine Vermentino, and dry spicy reds from a variety called Cannonau.

Campania, along with Puglia, makes some of the most exciting wine in the south of Italy. There are more than 100 grape varieties in Campania, including three of the south's most impressive ancient grapes: red Aglianico and two whites, Fiano and Greco, which thrive in the volcanic soils north-east of Mount Vesuvius.

Puglia's wine industry is also thriving, as old wineries have cleaned up their act. Investment is pouring in from well-known Italian producers further north, such as Tuscany's Antinori, while young guns make a name for themselves with the region's fascinating line-up of indigenous grape varieties. The leading varieties are Malvasia Nera di Brindisi, Nero di Troia and Primitivo, with Negroamaro taking the top spot in Puglia's most famous wine district, the Salento peninsula, where it makes happy-go-lucky Salice Salentino.

I've a particular passion for Sicilian wine – notably the wines from the brooding slopes around Mount Etna. The volcano might keep Sicilians awake at night with its regular pyrotechnics, but it has a giving side too, thanks to its rich volcanic soils and plentiful snowmelt – from intense pistachios and aromatic honeys to sweet, crunchy apples. Its jewel, though, is the wine – elegant, minerally reds and taut, tangy whites.

A quick scoot back up north, this time up the east coast, takes us to Abruzzo and the big red grape around these parts, Montepulciano. It varies hugely but shines in the wild hills around the town of Teramo, which has DOCG (denominazione di origine controllata e garantita) status for its Montepulciano d'Abruzzo Colline Teramane.

Volcano wine

Etna offers extreme winemaking in a unique microclimate, producing thrilling wines made from indigenous grapes. If Sicily feels like another country, far removed from the rolling hills of Tuscany, then Etna feels otherworldly, with its lunar landscapes and wildly unpredictable weather. Nowhere in Europe are the harvests so nerve-rackingly late, or at this elevation, with vines that average 100 years old or more, within sniffing distance of the sea. Nerello Mascalese is the big grape variety on Etna. It's often interplanted with Nerello Cappuccio and a smattering of other varieties, both red and white. Of the whites, Carricante is the standard-bearer, with a zesty bite.

Prosecco

After Abruzzo you hit the Marche
and Verdicchio country (or to
give it its full name, Verdicchio
dei Castelli di Jesi), which
are meaty but fresh whites.
Travel further north still
and you soon find yourself
in the Veneto, which has
a wealth of fine white
wines and some increasingly
accomplished reds. But I'm
going to focus on the most
popular wine of the far
eastern Veneto – Prosecco.
It's just an hour's drive from
Venice to the heart of Prosecco,
the pre-alpine hill country that
has brazenly nudged Champagne off
the top spot, making it the world's new
number one producer of sparkling wine. The
dramatic vine-clad foothills are dotted with imposing
Palladian palazzos, and great-value trattorias turning out the region's distinctive cuisine
for a fraction of the price offered in the famous lagoon nearby.

Even at the top end, at the very top level, single vineyard Prosecco won't break the
bank, and yes, before you ask, there is complexity to be had, even ageing potential, with
the best producers giving it their all – which includes working by hand in some of the
steepest vineyards in the world. You need to know, and most don't, that the really good
stuff comes from the steep slopes between Conegliano and Valdobbiadene and enjoys
DOCG status – so check for it on the label when you next buy a bottle.

Bàcari Crawl

'Eat where the locals eat and you can't
go wrong' is a maxim I follow keenly – and
nowhere more so than in Venice. Locals flock to
little bars called *bàcari*, where they eat *cicchetti*, small
snacks unique to Venice, washed down with a Prosecco,
or spritz. The best way to experience Venetian *bàcari* is on
a bar crawl, or *giro di ombre*. Start with a favourite, Naranzaria,
hidden on a quiet kink in the Grand Canal, where you can
nibble on artichoke *cicchetti* with your spritz and watch
the setting sun bounce off the crumbling palazzos. Then
decamp to the pavement terrace at Ostaria dai Zemei
for more stellar *cicchetti* (salt cod is a favourite),
before finishing at the city's oldest *bàcaro*,
the postage-stamp sized All'Arco. Want a
guide? Venice Bites offers spirited tours
(venicebitesfoodtours.com).

A LITTLE WORD ABOUT VERMOUTH, AND OTHER ITALIAN APERITIFS

Everybody is drinking vermouth these days, didn't you know? It was first created and sold in Piedmont in the 1700s. It fell out of favour for a while, but it's back – and on a café table near you, consumed solo, or mixed into various cocktails. It's a key ingredient in classics such as a Rob Roy and a Negroni (see page 136), or it can be sipped on its own with ice and a slice or twist of lemon or orange. What is it, exactly? Vermouth is a red or white wine infused with a blend of many different aromatic spices, barks, bitter herbs and other flavourings – Italian vermouth is sweet compared to French vermouth, which is dry. The big boys in Italian vermouth – Cinzano, Martini & Rossi and Punt e Mes – all have their headquarters around the Piedmont capital, Turin. Vying for similar attention on a Venetian pavement café is Aperol Spritz. Similar to Campari, though less bitter, Aperol is most commonly enjoyed over ice with Prosecco, a splash of soda and a slice of orange.

Black polenta, sun-dried tomato and mozzarella

I go to Venice for the bar food. Not the art, which is fabulous, or the palazzos, which are majestic, but the *cicchetti*. These small bites reign supreme in the *bàcari*, Venetian bars. It's where a Venetian goes to drink a spritz (between 6 and 8pm), a blend of Aperol or Campari and three-quarters Prosecco, topped up with a splash of soda water, served over ice with a slice of orange.

And with their spritz they eat *cicchetti*. These inventive morsels range from *polpettine di carne*, meat patties, and fat *tramezzini*, sandwiches bulging with stuffings such as tuna, egg and capers, plus lots of interesting things on toasted bread, with each *bàcaro* boasting its house special – from sea urchin and shredded lettuce to crab and radicchio. It's the ultimate bar food – so why not borrow a few ideas for the boat?

Bored with bread? Then try polenta. The instant stuff is perfect boat food, both bolstering and a great vehicle for strong flavours. I love it ramped up with squid ink stirred in while it's cooking (a Venetian thing). It cooks in no time and divvies up into neat little squares that will play piggyback to a host of different ingredients. I've chosen sun-dried tomato and mozzarella, but you can add Parma ham, too, or replace the mozzarella with feta cheese, add olives, cooked red peppers and many more.

Makes 9-10 bites

125g pre-cooked maize meal
  (polenta – the fast-cooking one)
2 x 4g sachets of squid ink
  (available in fishmongers)
140g jar of sun-dried tomatoes in oil, drained
150g mozzarella balls
salt and pepper

To serve:

cocktail sticks
basil leaves (optional)

Method

Bring 500ml water to the boil in a saucepan. Using a wooden spoon, stir in the maize meal and the squid ink, keep stirring over a low heat until it's nice and thick (about 5 minutes), and then season generously. Turn out on to a surface (use a baking tray or chopping board), spread into a rectangle about 2cm thick and leave to cool. Once cool, cut into bite-sized squares and top each with a piece of sun-dried tomato, then a mozzarella ball, and finally a basil leaf, if using, all secured with a cocktail stick. Serve with Prosecco, ideally.

Spain

Sherry

If I had to choose one region of Spain to hang out in, it would be Andalucía. Why? Sherry, in a word. And tapas, my favourite way to eat. Sitting in the main square in the seaside town of Sanlúcar de Barrameda with a glass of chilled manzanilla in one hand and a crunchy *tortillitas de camarones* (shrimp fritter) in the other is holiday heaven for me, so forgive the bias. Sherry is the undiscovered jewel of the wine world.

There are two basic styles: pale, delicate fino and manzanilla; and dark, nutty amontillado and oloroso. The Palomino grape rules here, and so does flor – the natural yeast that forms on the surface of the fino and manzanilla when in barrel. That's what gives the wine its unusual tang. When it has matured near the sea, as it is in Sanlúcar de Barrameda's manzanilla, the tang is even more pronounced (there's a great local aperitif to try with either, called a *rebujito*, a favourite at festivals, basically a sherry spritzer: serve long over ice topped up with lemonade or soda water).

Oloroso starts in the same way as these bone-dry sherries, but more fortifying alcohol is added before it is put into the barrel, after which it spends years darkening to a deep brown with concentrated, spicy wood flavours. It can be bottled dry or sweetened by the addition of concentrated grape juice. If you forget the years in barrel but do the rest, you get cream sherry, oloroso's much more economical cousin (try it on ice with a slice of orange for a zesty aperitif).

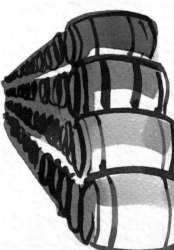

Wine

On the table-wine front, Spain has much to excite. Moving further around the coast, the vineyards inland from Spain's central Mediterranean coast have moved on at a cracking pace, with Denominación de Origens (DO) such as Alicante, Utiel-Requena with its fashionable Bobal grape, Valencia and Yecla making stylish, fruity reds, often blending local and international varieties.

Further north in Catalunya, or Catalonia, the range increases substantially, thanks to the huge difference in climates from the Mediterranean coast to the subalpine northern hills of the region.

There's cava, of course, Spain's answer to Champagne, produced on a fertile plateau in Penèdes, where lower yields and longer bottle ageing are improving things no end; and there are the still wines of Penèdes, which celebrate local Catalan grapes over international varieties, led by pioneer Miguel Torres.

For serious wine buffs there is also Priorat, whose muscular, pricey reds are made from grapes grown in dark brown slatey soil called llicorella. And not forgetting Empordà on the Costa Brava, the northernmost of Catalunya's DOs, that once produced crowd-pleasing pink wine but now turns out a growing range of well-made blends, both red and white.

Sailing into Mallorca? The past two decades have seen a revival in the wine industry here and both local and international grape varieties are now given the star treatment in the two DOs – Plà i Llevant to the east and Binissalem in the centre of the island.

Perfect Palma

With its palacios and promenades, chic restaurants and boutique hotels, Palma offers the boater a modern take on the Mallorcan capital's ancient past. Hire a bicycle or jump in a cab to the other side of Palma Bay to the colourful fishing village of Portixol, with its traditional *llaüts* (Mallorcan fishing boats) and busy harbour. Head to the stylish Portixol Hotel (portixol.com) where in-the-know locals come to sip early evening cocktails as the sun goes down on its waterside terrace, though I prefer to sip local whites such as aromatic Giró Blanc, an age-old Mallorcan variety made by Bodegas Can Majoral. Then nip next door to family-run Sa Roqueta for locally caught lobster rice.

Tuna-stuffed piquillo peppers

The Spanish are masters of superior tinned food, from meaty anchovies (Ortiz is a good brand) to more delicate Albacore tuna in extra virgin olive oil. It also does a great line in quality food in jars, from fat white asparagus, plucked from the plains of Navarra (try wrapping each stem in Serrano or Parma ham for another superior boat snack) to soft, nutty chickpeas, all of which will elevate your boat cooking in an instant.

My store cupboard is never without a jar or three of piquillo peppers. Piquillo means 'small beak' in Spanish, so called because of their tapered points. They are grown in Navarra, in the north of Spain, and have a sweet, smoky flavour. Picked at the end of the summer and into the autumn, they are grilled over charcoal and peeled by hand. Some supermarkets stock them, such as Waitrose, or they are available online from Spanish food stockists, such as brindisa.com. Failing that, use a jar of roasted red peppers, cut into inch-wide strips, which you can use to cover your tuna mixture.

For 4

1 x jar (220g drained)
  whole piquillo peppers
  – 12 in total
1 x 220g jar (150g drained)
  Albacore tuna in
  extra virgin olive oil
1 small shallot, finely
  chopped
1 tbsp capers, rinsed
  and chopped
3 tbsp flat-leaf parsley,
  chopped
2 tbsp extra virgin olive oil,
  plus extra for drizzling
½ lemon
salt and pepper

To serve:

12 slices of baguette,
  toasted
sea salt

Method

Place the tuna, shallot, capers, parsley and olive oil in a bowl. Squeeze over the lemon juice, season to taste and stir to combine. Gently stuff the mixture into the piquillo peppers. Arrange the baguette slices on a plate and top each one with a stuffed pepper. To serve, drizzle over a little olive oil and sprinkle with sea salt.

Croatia and Montenegro

Croatia

With 1,118 miles of coastline, and more than 1,000 islands, Croatia is a sailor's paradise – and now a wine drinker's paradise, too. Wine has been made here since 2,200 BC. The Greeks helped things along a bit, and later the Romans got stuck in – making wine purely for sacramental purposes, of course. But Ottoman invasions, world wars and the rise of communism slowed matters up somewhat. Things are back on track now, though, with newly designated wine regions.

For years, Croatian wine was divided into just two areas, Coastal and Continental. Then in 2012 a group of Croatian wineries, sommeliers and wine experts got together to create a new system that highlights four regions: Dalmatia, Istria and Kvarner, the Uplands, and Slavonia and Danube. These have been divided into 12 subregions, with 66 appellations between them.

Yes, wine is being made from international varieties, such as Cabernet Sauvignon, Chardonnay and Merlot, but Croatia boasts 64 indigenous varieties, which makes things significantly more exciting. It also has a tradition of making orange wines, now de rigueur on top wine lists, of which I'm a particular fan – white wines where the grape juice has been left in contact with the skins for a few days, weeks or even months, giving the finished wine an attractive orange hue.

To put things into perspective, there are now over 17,000 grape growers with more than 59,000 acres of vineyards, growing grapes for over 800 wineries. For me, Istria, sitting in the north-east corner of the country, just below Italy and Slovenia, is the jewel in the crown. The wine region includes the islands and the area surrounding the Kvarner Gulf, between the Istrian Peninsula and the mainland. Away from the pine-tree-studded, cove-lined coast, where most tourists head to, is a dramatic, picturesque tableau – think Tuscany 200 years ago, complete with crumbling hilltop villages, many of which have had a makeover.

Istria prides itself on being the gastronomic heart of Croatia, drawing influences from Italy to Hungary via Austria. It has a fabulous food culture (with white truffles at half the price you pay in Piedmont) and elegant wines. It was the first area in Croatia to see smart restaurants open their doors and the first to introduce a wine rating system and develop wine and olive oil routes.

Talking of wine, there is the honey-kissed, apple-skin-flavoured Malvasia Istriana, which is especially good when the grape skins have macerated in their juice, and another white variety called Zlahtina. The key red is Teran, plus the usual line-up of international varieties. There are many noteworthy producers, from Bruno Trapan to Ivica Matošević. And here's a bit of Istrian wine trivia for you – acacia is usually the barrel-wood of choice.

Montenegro

Neighbouring Montenegro's wine industry has also kept pace with the rise in tourism there – along with its play for the world's biggest superyachts, which increasingly reside in the Bay of Kotor's swanky Porto Montenegro marina.

The country has been making wine since Roman times. The dominant local grape variety, called Vranac (pronounced vrah-natz), is its biggest success story. Unlike many other grapes in the region (for example, Croatia's Plavac Mali, which is the same family as Italy's Primitivo and USA's Zinfandel), Vranac is unique. It's a thick-skinned dark grape and can be quite tannic, but it often benefits from some prolonged ageing – so don't be surprised if you see older vintages than you would expect on the shelves.

Plantaže is the name you will see most often – it's the largest producer and owner of one of Europe's biggest single vineyards. If the wines don't always reach the heights of what some independent producers can achieve in the best vintages, they are at least consistently good and offer excellent value (look out for its good-value Vranac Barrique).

The best Montenegrin wines, though, are being made by smaller producers, with retail prices ranging from €15 up to €50. Names to watch include Vinarija Krgović, with wines sold under the Arhonto brand, and Vinarija Vučinić, with its Zenta wines (both with vineyards near the Montenegrin capital, Podgorica), and Vinarija Milović, whose excellent Status is made from Vranac grapes grown in the southern coastal region, near Ulcinj, within sight of the Albanian border.

Wine buffs can be rather dismissive of the local white, Krstač (pronounced kris-tatch), though when I was there I happily downed a few bottles of it made by Plantaže in Montenegro's *konobas* (trattorias), where its herby, preserved lemon fruit and bracing acidity paired well with the garlicky flavours.

Greece

Wine

Greece is a great wine-producing region — it's just that we haven't discovered it yet. The names of the wines are a bit of a problem — Xinomavro and Malagousia don't exactly trip off the tongue like Chardonnay and Merlot. But get over it, get the bottles open and get tasting.

Greece practically invented winemaking, sure, but the new era for Greek wine, all agree, is when a handful of winemakers and agronomists returned home in the 1980s, after studying in France and California, to revitalise old-school wineries and get vineyards into shape, opening new ones along the way. Combine that with some serious investment, from both the EU and wealthy individuals, and you have an industry that has turned around — and could even help to dig Greece out of its current economic shambles.

The country has hundreds of different grape varieties, and some, such as Assyrtiko (remember its name), that may become world class. Here's a quick guide. Agiorgitiko is widely planted and makes smooth, full-bodied, easy-drinking reds. It shines in the northern half of the Peloponnese, which has seen more quality wine action than anywhere else in Greece in recent years. Neméa in the east is the most important appellation and makes luscious reds from the grape.

Limnio is another key red grape. It's often blended, but on its own produces herbaceous wines with a kick. Xinomavro is also popular – planted in the north, it makes high-acidity wines with

an appealing savouriness. There are also plantings of French varieties, such as Grenache, Cabernet Sauvignon and Merlot.

On the white grape front, as well as Assyrtiko there is the light-bodied, aromatic Moschfilero, and the full-bodied, fresh Roditis, which is widely planted.

Where are the vineyards? In every region, though Greece is mostly mountainous and infertile so the combination of high altitudes, steep slopes, complex topography and unpredictable rainfall make this some of the most demanding terroir in the world to work in.

There's Macedonia in the north, where you'll find Náoussa, the most important (and first) appellation established in 1971, making reds with serious ageing potential. Then there are the Ionian Islands in the west and Crete to the south, which has been enjoying its own wine revolution, and the Aegean islands to the east. But it's in the southern Aegean that you'll find volcanic Santorini and some of the best Assyrtiko. The vines are trained in little nests that hunker down out of the wind on the slopes of a dormant volcano. The resulting wines show a stunning complexity and a salty crispness that will have you sailing back for more. Highlights include Gaia's Thalassitis and Sigalas.

While you are skitting around the Aegean, you could also check out the sweet wines made of Muscat produced in several islands. Sámos makes the best, even oak-ageing some of them with good results.

Ouzo

And we can't leave Greece without a quick word about ouzo. What is it? Ouzo is made from the spent grape skins *et al* from winemaking, then distilled and flavoured primarily with anise. It's part of a family of drinks common to countries with a strong Muslim influence, known as arak in Lebanon and raki in Turkey – don't forget Greece was once part of the Ottoman Empire. How to drink ouzo? Place one or two ice cubes into a small glass and pour over a small amount of ouzo. Sip slowly, accompanied by a small plate or two of *mezedes* – it works particularly well with grilled octopus, prawns and squid.

Feta and olive bites

I first made a version of these soon after I got my hands on Honey & Co's debut cookbook. The Honeys, as I call them, are husband and wife team Itamar Srulovich and Sarit Packer, who run one of my favourite London restaurants, Honey & Co. With its whitewashed walls and Moorish tiled floor, it has a Levantine menu that truly excites. The tiny room and raised decibels just add to the fun. I've cooked these warm cheesy things from the Balkans (where they're called *bouikos*) again and again, on the boat, too – simplifying an already simple recipe that takes moments to

throw together. I've substituted some ingredients to make it more boat-friendly, replacing the Cheddar and spring onions with more resilient Parmesan and black olives – though if you aren't using marinated olives you could add half a garlic clove, crushed, and a pinch of dried thyme. When I make them at home I do as Sarit suggests and freeze them for later use, defrosting them for half an hour before cooking and scoffing while still warm. In place of olives, you could use finely chopped sun-dried tomatoes.

Makes 16-20

50g cold butter
40g Parmesan
40g feta
100g plain flour
50ml sour cream or full-fat
 Greek yoghurt
2 tbsp chopped marinated,
 pitted black olives

Method

Preheat the oven to 200°C/fan 180°C/gas 6. Cut the butter into small dice. Grate the Parmesan and crumble the feta, then with your hands mix all the ingredients straight away, working the dough as little as possible until it just combines – you want oozing lumps of butter and cheese. Place the dough on a lightly floured surface and pat it into a rough rectangle 2–3cm thick, then cut it into small triangles using a floured knife (you should get around 16–20). Bake on a non-stick baking tray for 15 minutes, or until golden. Eat straight away or cool on the tray until serving. Best eaten on the same day.

Turkey

Wine

People in Turkey don't drink a lot of wine. Tourists, yes – they account for nearly half the consumption. If the Turks are going to drink, they are more likely to have a beer or a glass of raki (see below). That's if they drink at all – so not a great incentive to transform the wine industry, then. Things are changing though. Two big privately owned wine companies basically run the show in Turkey, Doluca and Kavaklidere. The rest is mainly made up of smaller 'boutique' producers, which are growing at a steady pace.

The main wine regions are Thrace, in the European bit of Turkey, located to the west and north of Istanbul; the mild Aegean coast and its hinterland; around Tokat, north of the capital Ankara; Cappadocia in central Anatolia; eastern Anatolia; and south-eastern Anatolia, which borders Iran.

There are minimal wine laws in Turkey compared with the main wine-producing regions – so anything goes. For me, there are too many wines made from international grapes that are a tad heavy on the oak and high on the alcohol – but they like it that way, they will argue. The blends with international and local grapes are much more interesting, such as Chardonnay and Narince, the latter a key ingredient in the Turkish national dish, *dolma* – stuffed vine leaves.

In fact, it's the indigenous grapes that excite the most – my favourite Turkish wine is made by the Vinkara winery near Ankara, using a local tongue-twister of a grape called Kalecik Karasi. Other indigenous grapes include Öküzgözü and Emir. Want to give them a try? Get in touch with Mark Hopkins at tasteturkey.net.

How to drink raki like a Turk

Raki is serious business in Turkey. It's the go-to spirit for celebrations, and a raki-fuelled night often ends with dancing on the table. Raki always sparks soulful discussions and it's part of the country's psyche. What's it made of? Like Greek ouzo, it's distilled using the leftover grapes from winemaking and flavoured primarily with anise. How to drink raki? A group of novices should ask for a 35cl bottle and tell the waiter that you each want a *tek* (4cl), which is about one shot. Seasoned raki drinkers often have a double (8cl). After pouring the raki, the waiter will ask if you want water and ice – say yes to both. Though some raki aficionados will tell you that ice dilutes the flavour. To make a toast with raki, clink the bottom of the glass – touching the top means you think you are better than them. Another cute raki tradition is to knock your glass lightly on the table after toasting in remembrance of someone you wish was present. *Serefinize*! (Cheers!)

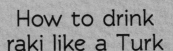

Ask most people what Baltic booze means to them and they'll reply vodka, or aquavit, and beer, of course – everywhere makes beer. But there are many more drinks to explore here.

There are vineyards in Denmark – bet you didn't know that. How about a cheeky bottle of Rondo, or Solaris, as you watch the sun go down in Bornholm after a day on the water? There are now more than 55 wine producers in Denmark, so remember that the next time you reach for a bottle of identikit New World Cabernet Sauvignon here.

Neighbouring Sweden also likes a drink. Again, vodka and aquavit rule, and like Denmark, it also has a burgeoning wine industry, growing grapes such as Vidal (though I'm rather partial to a glass of Sav, sparkling birch sap, which is made in Östersund – but that's another story). The Swedes famously like a singsong when they drink, so I've helpfully included one for you, which should make you feel right at home.

Russia and vodka are, of course, inextricably linked – beer wasn't considered alcohol until 2013. But there is life beyond the scarily potent 'water of life' – meet a rather delicious low-alcohol alternative called kvas, made from fermented dark rye bread (you have to be there).

Germany might seem like an odd addition in this chapter, but it does have a Baltic coastline, and while its vineyards are many miles further south, it does make some of the world's greatest white wines, and some pretty fine beer, so its inclusion is a no-brainer. Roll with it.

Denmark

Beer

When most people think of Danish booze, they think of beer. This is the home of Carlsberg, after all, one of the biggest beer brands in the world. Beer has been part of Danish culture for over 5,000 years and they drink a fair amount of it, along with the rest of the world, who import it by the container-load.

Until 1830, the only beer produced in Denmark was *hvidtøl*, white beer, but that year a brewer called JC Jacobsen presented the Danish king with a new type of beer, Bavarian lager, which had a finer flavour and a longer shelf life. Cue Carlsberg, and later Skol, owned by Carlsberg Breweries.

Denmark is also home to the Tuborg brewery, founded in 1873, which introduced a Pilsner-style lager to the Danes. This is still the dominant beer style in Denmark, but in the last couple of decades over 200 microbreweries have been established offering many different styles, with Amager Bryghus leading the way.

Aquavit

When the Danes aren't drinking beer, they're drinking aquavit. The name means 'water of life', and it's basically a distilled spirit made from grain or potatoes, much like vodka. Aquavit's distilling history dates back to 1400, and by the mid-19th century large-scale distilling had begun. The biggest brand is Aalborg, named after a small town in Jutland on Denmark's northern coast.

What sets aquavit apart from other similar spirits is the addition of distilled extracts of a range of herbs and spices,

How to drink aquavit like a Dane

Say aquavit – or 'snaps' – to a Danish bartender and you'll trigger a little ritual. A cone-shaped frosted glass about the size of a large thimble is plucked from the freezer. Aquavit from a similarly chilled bottle is then poured to the rim. To complete the ritual, look your drinking partner in the eye, down it in one – then shout a hearty *'Skoal!'*

with caraway the most common flavouring. But dill, coriander, citrus and cinnamon are also used.

How to drink it? Usually with food, and usually with a beer chaser. It goes particularly well with marinated and pickled herring, salads and cold meats. For a great aquavit experience, head to the Danish island of Bornholm, to the oldest smokehouse in Gudhjem, one of the harbour towns on the north coast, where the aquavit is served with herrings that are dried for 90 minutes and then smoked over alder wood until golden.

Wine

Incredibly, wine is also produced in Denmark. A 15-minute drive from the centre of Copenhagen will take you to one of the first vineyards in the country, Dansk Vincenter. Established in 1999 by a former market gardener, Torben Andreasen, it produces up to 7,000 bottles a year. Andreasen wanted to prove that it was possible to produce wine here. Now others have joined him, and there are more than 55 wine producers in Denmark today. And no, the climate hasn't suddenly warmed up here – they've just been a bit clever with the varieties, using red grapes such as Rondo and Castel and white grapes such as Solaris and Orion, which suit the cooler climate.

Germany

Wine

If you're cruising the north coast of Germany and its islands you will want to drink German wine. Why? Because the country makes some of the world's best white wines. When it's good – and there's a lot that is good here – it has a vibrancy, racy elegance, perfume and freshness that is hard to beat.

Not that you will get a chance to visit its vineyards if you are sailing in the north, there aren't any up here – Germany's vineyards are much further south. Not that you can describe it as the south, exactly. Many of Germany's best vineyards are planted about as far north as grapes will ripen, with some of the best grapes planted on land that is good for nothing else, thanks to the staggering steepness of the slopes.

Your experience of German wine is Liebfraumilch? The less said about Liebfraumilch the better. It's a part of Germany's winemaking history that is best forgotten, and it was damaging both to its reputation and, ultimately, its export market. No, things have changed a lot here in recent years.

Thanks to climate change, grapes consistently ripen fully here, and Germany's sweet wines are even more ambrosial than ever, because of that ripeness. But because we don't drink much sweet wine, producers focus mostly on dry wines, from spätlese to the best wines from the best vineyards, labelled grosses gewächs.

So what to drink? Riesling, in a word. It reigns supreme here. The country's best wines are made from Riesling grapes (pronounced rees-ling) and they range from steely and dry, laced with apples and apricots, to richly honeyed, bursting with pineapple, peach and mango flavours, a satisfying twist of lime on the finish. The drier styles are spectacular with a vast range of food.

After Riesling, the next most widely planted grape variety is Müller-Thurgau. It lacks Riesling's backbone of fruity acidity but it ripens earlier and it's a mainstay of German plonk production. Silvaner, meanwhile, is the third most planted grape variety, but while it lags far behind the other two in terms of numbers, it shines in spots like Franken, where it revels in the clay limestone soils. Other key German grapes include Grauburgunder (Pinot Gris) and Weissburgunder (Pinot Blanc), which flourish in Baden and some sites in the Pfalz.

There has also been a significant rise in planting of red varieties in Germany, with much excitement now surrounding these wines, most notably those made of Spätburgunder (Pinot

Noir), plantings of which have tripled in recent years, and Dornfelder, which makes appealing reds in the Pfalz. In fact, over 35 per cent of all Germany's vineyards are now planted with red wine grapes.

So where are the vineyards, exactly? Germany's reputation as the world's greatest white wine producer was historically based on the Rheingau, a south-facing stretch of vineyards producing mainly Riesling on gentle slopes leading down to the Rhine. And thrilling wines are still produced here. The Rheingau takes the prize for the most exciting and inventive wine region in Germany, and its winemakers are making more great wines from different types of grapes than any other place in the country, thanks to the wide variety of soils and its sunny latitude. The best have a creamy acidity and an impressive vibrancy.

The Rheinessen, south of the Rheingau, is Germany's largest wine area. This is Liebfraumilch country, but don't let that put you off – the region makes some fabulous Rieslings and serious Scheurebe.

The Mosel is where Germany's sexiest wines are made. The wine region is defined by the Mosel River, which weaves majestically through a valley carved out in craggy mountains 400 million years ago and now banked by jaw-droppingly steep vineyards.

Other regions of note include Nahe, south of the Mosel, Mittelrhein (middle Rhine), Baden, Franken and Ahr.

Hop to it

It's not all about wine in Germany – the country also makes a huge range of beer. In fact, there are around 5,000 different beers to choose from, brewed by more than 1,300 breweries, over half of which are in Bavaria. Although Bavaria in the south is the spiritual home of the German beer garden, there are a few beer gardens in northern, coastal Hamburg for the boater to try, such as Schuhmachers at the head of the Stadtparksee. Germany might not have invented beer, but it has a long brewing history that dates back over 3,000 years. And they take it very seriously indeed – a beer purity law introduced in 1487 ruled that only barley, hops and water could be used to make beer. That law survived until the 1990s, but many brewers are still faithful to it.

Sweden

Vodka

The Swedes like a drink. And they have many drinking traditions, and drinking songs – more of which later. But according to their government, they love their drink just a bit too much, so it introduced a state monopoly to control the production and sale of all alcoholic beverages and raised taxes to astronomical levels. I mention this now because it plays a huge factor in their drinking history.

Though it's not like it held the Swedes back. They just started to make their own booze, or piled on to duty-free ferry routes between countries to enjoy a tipple, or slipped over to Denmark to have a drink or three. But out of this tight control came one of the world's biggest spirit brands – Absolut Vodka.

It was after one such crackdown – the first of many attempts by the Swedish government to exert control over consumption – that Lars Olsson Smith, Sweden's most famous distiller, emerged on to the scene. He created the country's first rectified spirit in 1879, and was so convinced that his Absolut Rent Brannvin (Absolutely Pure Vodka) was the very best vodka on the market that he took on the might of the Stockholm monopoly.

Smith's distillery was located just outside Stockholm's city limits – and therefore outside its jurisdiction. He provided a free ferry service to his establishment, and his customers couldn't get enough of his vodka. When he needed to buy more raw material to meet the increasing demand, Smith switched production to southern Sweden, buying up distilleries and making sure his vodka had the widest distribution in the land. The government responded by raising taxes and taking over control of all vodka sales. Absolut was virtually forgotten about until 1979, when the state decided to release it on to the international market and it went on to become one of the biggest brands in the world.

Not that vodka is the number one drink in Sweden – that's beer. Up until recently we were talking lager from larger breweries, followed by a flood of imports (the Swedes love American beer). But in the 1990s a handful of pioneers began opening their own breweries, which enjoyed steady growth. Fast-forward to today and that growth has become an explosion, with microbreweries popping up all over Sweden, including FemAle, who recently launched Sweden's first beer brewed by and for women – a pale ale called We Can Do It.

Beware: drinking in Sweden can be expensive. Though there are ways of softening the blow – either bypass the bars and buy your own booze from the state-run booze shops called *Systembolaget*, or just stick to happy hour.

Coffee

Coffee, too, is big in Sweden. The time set aside for drinking coffee even has a special name – *fika* – and it is part of everyday life. But it's not just about the coffee – it's a chance to slow down and appreciate the good things in life – ideally with a cinnamon bun in your other hand.

Aquavit

And, of course, let's not forget aquavit – or snaps, as they call it. Similar to Danish aquavit, the spirit is distilled from grain or potatoes, but the Swedish version can have pronounced fennel, anise and citrus flavours. And like the Danes, the Swedes serve it chilled in small, stemmed glasses and down it in one gulp, often followed by a beer.

A song for snaps

The Swedes have a tendency to burst into song before downing a shot of snaps, and they keep on singing with increasing enthusiasm with each round of shots. It's especially popular during crayfish season in August and September, when people wear silly hats and eat copious amounts of the prized, pricey shellfish. There are more than 9,000 drinking songs recorded at the Museum of Spirits in Stockholm (spritmuseum.se), and more than 200 of them are for snaps.

Swedish drinking song:

Herring and sill

You can give us herring
And you can give us sill
But you will still be erring
Unless you also will
Give us a glass of aquavit
That sure smells sweet
To Swedes in heat
It gives the fish its feet
It makes the dish complete.

Gravadlax and beetroot

One of the best fast foods on the planet, gravadlax is fresh salmon cured for a couple of days with a winning mix of dill, sea salt, sugar and pepper. You can make your own but there are plenty of good-quality shop-bought ones around – they even come with their own sweet mustard sauce, though making your own sauce ahead of things takes it to another level. In her brilliant book *Scandilicious*, my Norwegian friend, Signe Johansen, offers an easy recipe that works particularly well. Simply whizz up a 50g pack of fresh dill, stalks removed, 2 tbsp each of vegetable oil, white wine or cider vinegar, demerara sugar, and Dijon mustard with a pinch of salt and it's ready to use, and keeps for a week in the fridge in an airtight jar. You can use those long-life packs of pumpernickel for this, cut into four canapé-sized squares, but I'm rather partial to Peter's Yard crispbread, available in Waitrose and online, which also come in handy bite-sized pieces – perfect for a boat nibble.

For 4

12 bite-size Swedish-style crispbreads, or 4 large crispbreads
butter, for spreading
145g gravadlax (or 4 slices)
sweet mustard sauce (see above)
4 tbsp beetroot, chopped (either pickled or in their own juice, whatever you prefer)

To serve:

dill fronds, if you want to be a bit fancy

Method

Butter the crispbreads and divide up the salmon between them, drizzling over the mustard sauce and scattering the beetroot. Dot dill fronds over the top and eat immediately.

Russia

Vodka

Most people think Russia invented vodka. After all, the word comes from the Russian *zhiznennia voda*, which means 'water of life' (or translated literally, 'little water'). But Russia didn't invent vodka – Poland did. The evidence suggests that the Poles picked up distilling techniques from the West and it spread from there into Russia and the Baltic States. Yet Russia and vodka are inextricably linked.

Russia is still the largest vodka market in the world. They guzzle a billion litres of it a year, according to recent figures. That's almost a third of global consumption. The downside is that their high alcohol consumption has long been linked to Russia's high mortality rates – but let's not spoil a good party. The Russians have been making an effort to address this, thanks to tighter alcohol restrictions and higher taxes (beer wasn't even classed as an alcoholic drink until 2013), and they are drinking less as each year passes.

So when did the Russians start making vodka? Around the mid-15th century, say some. Peter the Great (1672–1725) liberalised distillation – mainly to collect taxes, but vodka production back then was essentially a rich man's hobby. By the middle of the 17th century every nobleman was producing his own brand of vodka, and by the 18th century Russia was awash with posh-boy brands, which began to acquire an international reputation.

Everyone else, meanwhile, was drinking crude spirits made from potato, beet and nettles, bought at bargain basement prices from Poland, Germany, and

from illicit stills. The state responded by taking control of production and introducing quality control – thanks to a St Petersburg boffin called Dr Mendeleev, who discovered a method, still used today, of purifying alcohol using charcoal filtration.

We have the Russian Revolution to thank, in part, for the explosion in vodka distilleries in other countries. After the Bolsheviks confiscated distilleries in Moscow, producers emigrated, taking their recipes with them – including one Vladimir Smirnov, founder of the Smirnoff distillery.

Alternatives

There is life beyond vodka in Russia. They actually make some pretty decent beer, such as Vasileostrovskaya Pivovarnya in St Petersburg. And they love a cuppa – always served black, sometimes with a little sugar, no milk.

Another low- or no-alcohol alternative is kvas, basically a beer made from fermented dark rye bread. It's the old proletariat brew – farmers and workers used to drink it instead of water to quench their thirst. It's best quaffed straight from a street vendor on a hot summer's day. Mors is also a delicious, non-alcoholic alternative – a sweet juice-like drink made from fermented bilberries.

When it's cold, wet and grey, I picture this – a warm sandy beach at sunset, surfers riding the waves, a cold bottle of craft beer in my hand. In fact, that's an image you can repeat all over the Pacific, from San Diego to Sydney. Even Singapore has a craft beer scene (albeit artificial waves).

San Diego in California is the world capital of the craft beer scene; sail 184 nautical miles north and you're in thrilling wine country. California's Central Coast region is home to some great winemakers turning out interesting wines that give venerable Napa a run for its money.

And I have to give a big nod to British Columbia wine while we're out West – it's tried so hard over the last few decades, and is succeeding in the most part, plus the scenery in Okanagan is stunning. Combine the two, and what's not to like?

Keep heading west and you'll hit another sailing (and drinking) hot spot, Hong Kong. And no, they haven't started planting vineyards here, but they do know how to do happy hour – and rooftop cocktail bars. Ditto Singapore.

Head down a bit, and left a bit, and you'll hit Australia. What has happened to the wine scene in Oz in the last few decades is astonishing, shaking up an industry that needed taking down a peg or two, with the best yet to come.

Finally, New Zealand. Remote outpost it may be, but there's nothing far flung about its wine scene. It owns Sauvignon Blanc, putting the grape on the map worldwide. But it now also makes fine Chardonnay, elegant Pinot Noir, and Riesling that will knock your socks off. Enjoy the ride.

Australia

Wine

The last time I visited Australia I ate a poisonous leaf. 'Don't worry, when you cook it the toxins are released,' grinned Adelaide chef Dennis Leslie. The deep-fried saltbush was sitting on my kangaroo steak, which had been rubbed with ground pepperberries. It was served with bush tomatoes and warrigal greens and then finished with quandong and desert lime sauce. Welcome to Australia.

I'm glad they are getting to know their indigenous ingredients. They've been getting to know what grape varieties grow best where, too, since they planted the first vines in 1791. That's something we should know, but most of us don't.

We love Australian wines, the Brits in particular – one in every five bottles of wine we drink is Australian. But do we know – or even care – where that bottle came from exactly? Most of us don't – and it's the Aussies' fault. They have done such a good job of shaking up the industry over the last 25 years by persuading us that it was more important to know the name of the grape variety than where it was grown that we just went with the flow, relieved that we no longer had to stare vacantly at complicated and unpronounceable appellations on wine labels, enjoying the fat, fruity ride.

But the Australians have changed tack in recent years. They want us to take their regional differences much more seriously. The word 'terroir', coyly avoided until recently by so many of Australia's winemaking fraternity, has been taken up with gusto by many. They want us to know that the Margaret River region is really good at Cabernet and Chardonnay; that the Clare Valley is perfect for Riesling; and that the Barossa is not just one big bowl of Shiraz.

Indeed, one look at the official map and you'll clock that there are more than 60 designated wine regions across the country. Suddenly, Australia looks a lot more complex and interesting, doesn't it? In fact, as well as regional distinction, the focus is now on the country's subregions and single vineyards, which draw attention to specific sites – so-called 'block' wines, at the high end at least. In short, these days there are many Australian wines that show their origin.

Though that's not to say that Australian winemakers still aren't routinely revelling in their freedom to plant what they want, where they want – freedom European winemakers just don't have. They are, and we are glad they are – Aussie Arneis, anyone? The best is certainly yet to come from Australia, as winemakers further understand their vineyards and soils, even in the most established wine regions.

Bung me a tinny, mate

After wine, beer is the number one glug in Oz ('tinny' is slang for beer in cans). It used to be the most popular drink, until wine took over in the 1970s. The settlers brought rum and beer with them back in the day and were soon producing it themselves. In fact, rum was such a valued commodity that it became the key currency in the early years. Some of those early breweries are still in production, including Cascade Brewery in Tasmania, established in 1824, and the only remaining family-owned brewery, Coopers, in South Australia, which started trading in 1862. Not forgetting Fosters, in Melbourne, which began life in 1867. Ginger beer was also a thing here, bottled in stoneware in the 1820s for both convicts and the public, with ginger beer breweries from Bundaberg to Broome. The potteries could barely keep up with demand – and it remained popular until the 1940s.

TEN KEY AUSTRALIAN WINE REGIONS TO EXPLORE NEAR THE COAST

1 Barossa

Drive an hour north-east from Adelaide and you will find the epicentre of Australian wine. More wine is made in the Barossa than in any other region and it boasts a rich viticultural history. The industry's past, present and future are all on show here, from its gnarled 100-year-old, bush-pruned Shiraz to spindly, young Nebbiolo.

2 Shoalhaven Coast

This fast-developing wine country stretches from Kiama in the north to Durras in the south and west to Kangaroo Valley on the south coast of New South Wales. Think luscious green valleys, pristine beaches and a plethora of exciting new varieties, such as Arneis and Tannat.

3 Margaret River

This far-western region, south of Perth, has notched up many awards for its powerful yet elegant Cabernets, stunning Sauvignon Blancs and classy Chardonnays. Its vineyards are cooled by the stiff breezes of the Indian Ocean – much to the delight of the area's many surfing winemakers. Not bad, considering it was only 'discovered' as a great grape-growing area in the 1970s.

4 Adelaide Hills

Head east out of Adelaide and 20 minutes' drive later you'll hit the hills. Surprisingly unspoiled, this cool-climate area (with a few warm pockets) excels in Pinot Noir and Chardonnay, where grapes from the coolest sites are destined for some pretty fine bubbly. It also produces benchmark Sauvignon Blanc.

5 McLaren Vale

One of Australia's greenest wine regions, McLaren Vale is located in South Australia, nestled between the Mount Lofty Ranges and the beaches of Gulf St Vincent. It produces some of the country's richest, silkiest reds, from varieties such as Shiraz and Grenache. Rolling hills, rugged coast, charming villages – what's not to like?

6 Coonawarra

Found in the far south-east of South Australia, Coonawarra has been making wine since 1890. Cabernet Sauvignon is the big thing here, made from grapes grown in the region's famous rich, red soil (*terra rossa*), which helps to give the wines character, finesse and great ageing potential.

7 Tasmania

With its mild summers and long autumn days, this unique island state provides elegant cool climate wines such as Pinot Noir, sparkling wines, Riesling and Chardonnay.

8 Mornington Peninsula

Boutique wineries rule here, producing a dizzying array of different wines made on different sites. The bucolic, cool-climate region also doubles up as a fashionable seaside destination.

9 Great Southern

Pounded by the Southern Ocean and steeped in settler history, the Great Southern is aptly named. The region was instrumental in establishing modern winemaking in Western Australia in the 1960s.

10 Hunter Valley

The Hunter Valley is the most famous wine region in New South Wales. Hunter's humid climate produces plump, juicy Shiraz and a wide range of whites, including the region's long-ageing Sémillons.

New Zealand

There was a time when I couldn't drink anything else. Back in the 1980s, New Zealand Sauvignon Blanc offered a treasure trove of new flavours, with its gooseberry fruit and bracing acidity. The country made its name on the back of it, and still does, with plenty of fans, some of whom will happily pay over the odds for the king of New Zealand Sauvignon Blanc, Cloudy Bay.

One of the world's most successful wine brands, Cloudy Bay helped to launch an entire region, putting Marlborough and New Zealand on the map. Its success is down to a combination of factors – but top of that list is a distinctive Sauvignon Blanc and an exclusivity that created demand. And we still can't get enough New Zealand Sauvignon Blanc, paying nearly £2 per bottle more than the average.

The Marlborough region owns Sauvignon Blanc. It plants more than the whole of France put together and accounts for the majority of New Zealand's plantings. You can thank the alluvial loam over deep deposits of gravel, and the staggered picking (different levels of ripeness add complexity to the finished wine), plus better clones and some strategic leaf plucking. Among my favourites are Isabel, Greywacke and Seresin.

But New Zealand is by no means a one-trick pony. The buzzword in the wine world right now is diversity and New Zealand can deliver that too, with fine Chardonnays, elegant Pinot Noirs, and many more. Pinot Noir in particular has had a stellar rise to fame here, while Pinot Gris and Riesling are also causing a stir.

Magical Martinborough

Just over an hour from Wellington, with its own exciting craft beer scene, is the buzzy wine town of Martinborough. Its streets take the shape of the Union Jack, meeting in the centre to form a pretty square. Wellingtonians flock here at the weekends, along with scores of wine tourists, to colonise the chic B&Bs and smart restaurants staffed by innovative chefs. They come for the wine, too – for the elegant Pinot Noir, which vies for supremacy over that other Pinot hot spot, Central Otago, and they come for its Pinot Gris, New Zealand's latest varietal sensation. This area of the Wairarapa wine region has poor soils and prevailing westerlies – manna for your ambitious winemaker, who will tell you that it's just like Burgundy. There are over 20 largely family-owned wineries to work your way around – my picks include Ata Rangi, Craggy Range, Martinborough Vineyard and Palliser Estate. For a more structured wine trail, visit winesfrommartinborough.com.

Stuffed mussels with parsley, garlic and Parmesan

The small New Zealand town of Havelock is the green shell mussel capital of the world. It's located in the Marlborough region on the South Island and each year it plays host to a festival that celebrates the country's highly prized shellfish. Thousands come to shuck, stuff, and savour the mussels, with their mild, sweet flavour. And get this, the green shell mussel, also known as the green lipped mussel, has healing properties, too. It's supposed to help relieve the pain of arthritis, thanks to its high levels of omega-3 fatty acids – something the Maoris noticed more than a century ago. They're not so easy to get hold of outside the country, so ordinary farmed mussels will do for this recipe. To match? A Marlborough Sauvignon Blanc, of course.

For 4

1 kg mussels
splash of white wine
40g fresh breadcrumbs
2 tbsp finely chopped
   flat-leaf parsley
3 garlic cloves, crushed
4 tbsp grated Parmesan
4 tbsp extra virgin olive oil
salt and pepper

To serve:

lemon wedges

Method

Wash the mussels in cold water and pull off their beards. Discard any with damaged shells or that don't shut immediately when sharply tapped. Bring 100ml water to the boil with the white wine in a saucepan. Add the mussels and simmer for 3–4 minutes. Drain and discard any mussels that remain shut. Discard the empty half shells and place the mussels in their shell in an ovenproof dish. Preheat the grill. Combine the breadcrumbs, parsley, garlic, cheese and olive oil in a bowl and season to taste. Scatter over the mussels in their shells. Grill for 6–8 minutes or until the topping is lightly browned. Garnish with the lemon wedges and serve hot, straight from the dish.

Canada

The Canadians are pretty new at this winemaking lark. And no, before you ask, it isn't too cold to make wine here – its major wine regions are on the same latitude as some key European vineyards.

Their wine industry seems to have sprung out of nowhere. It's proper pioneer stuff, and impressive when you count the medals being scooped at wine competitions. It's not a huge industry – Canada has less than the grape acreage of Switzerland, for example, but it has moved on at a cracking pace. In a ten-year period, the number of wineries has quadrupled.

Its two most important wine regions are on opposite sides of the country. Ontario in the east, principally the Niagara Peninsula, and British Columbia in the west, mainly the Okanagan Valley. And as the Okanagan Valley is the most accessible for the boater, both to buy and drink in bars on the Canadian west coast, and to visit (it's a stunning four-hour drive over dramatic mountains from Vancouver, or a short flight), this is what I'm going to focus on.

Okanagan is one of the most northerly wine regions. Close your eyes, sip a glass of Okanagan Riesling and you could be in the Mosel; and its best Pinot Noir bears more than just a passing resemblance to Burgundy.

The Okanagan Valley extends for 150 miles with wineries and towns running up and down the length of the lake. And what a lake. Many of the 170 or so wineries look out on to the glittering water, with its mountainous backdrop of extinct volcanos. Add to that a growing number of excellent winery restaurants, such as the Sonora Room at the Burrowing Owl Winery, plus a plethora of boutique hotel accommodation, and you have yourself a perfect break from the ocean. Other top producers to visit include Sumac Ridge, Meyer Family, Quails' Gate, Mission Hill and Gray Monk.

They first grew grapes in the Okanagan Valley back in the 1860s for sacramental wine purposes. But the industry didn't amount to much, thanks to a complex series of political and economic barriers, including the creation of government monopolies to control the sale and distribution of booze. It wasn't until the early 1990s that its modern wine industry took off. Canada now makes world-class Riesling, Chardonnay, Pinot Noir and Cabernet Franc. Insider tip – it also makes ethereal ice wines that will blow your mind (and your wallet) and have become the country's calling card, made by picking the frozen grapes off the vine in deep winter.

Each part of the valley has its own unique terroir and favoured grape varieties, which means Okanagan is suited to an unusually varied selection of varietals, offering a range of different flavours. And though white grapes took the lead here in the early days, red varieties such as Pinot Noir, Merlot, Cabernet Sauvignon, Cabernet Franc, Malbec and Syrah have caught up.

Climate-wise, it's a winemaker's paradise. Expect scant rainfall, consistently sunny days and super-cool nights, which means lots of fruit, and lots of balancing, zippy acidity. It might not be far from the Pacific Ocean as the crow flies, but it's sheltered behind the Coastal Range so it can get extremely warm here – did I mention the time I stumbled across a rattlesnake in a vineyard here? That's another story.

Hong Kong

At first glance, Hong Kong is overwhelming. You'll spend the first couple of days just gawping at the architecture, from majestic older buildings to glittering skyscrapers. But once you've spent a little time here you'll realise that its main appeal is how this island city has managed to balance a modern way of life with strong cultural traditions.

Your first port of call is likely to be the Royal Hong Kong Yacht Club. Voted Best Asian Yacht Club, it's one of the oldest sports clubs in Hong Kong and it's proud of its rich colourful history, which stretches back over 160 years. It has three clubhouses: its main base on Kellett Island, with sweeping views over the city; Middle Island, on the south side; and Shelter Cove, in a picturesque bay in Sai Kung.

Most who sail through here will hit the bar at some point. Ask bartender Ben to mix you up a club special, the Gunner (see page 161), or, if it's chilly, ask for a Hoi Loong, which takes its name from a Dragon class boat that belonged to Pat Loseby, the first lady Vice Patron of the RHKYC. This is her recipe, conceived after a cold day on the water. In a mug, mix equal parts of dark rum and orange and lemon cordials, and top with hot water. Loseby used to take a Thermos flask of ready-mixed Hoi Loong with her on sailing trips to Junk Bay, Port Shelter and her favourite anchorage, Big Snake Bay.

And when you're not on the water, or in the bar at the RHKYC, then you'll be hitting the lights and heights of Hong Kong (rooftop cocktail bars are a big thing here). So what to drink? Or rather make that, what to eat and drink – as locals can't do one without the other. I'm talking tea and dim sum.

Going out for dim sum is known as *yum cha*, which literally means 'drinking tea'. It's a way of life here and a must-do when in Hong Kong. A particular favourite is Tim Ho Wan in Kowloon – touted as the cheapest Michelin-starred restaurant in the world (but there are other branches here, and many more abroad, such is the demand for its outstanding cooking).

Forget coffee, it's all about milk tea for your caffeine hit in Hong Kong. About 900 million glasses of milk tea are downed each year. Made with strong black tea and condensed milk, it's served in local *cha chan tengs* across the city.

TOP FIVE BARS TO WATCH THE SUNSET IN HONG KONG

1 Ozone at Ritz-Carlton
The world's highest rooftop bar on the 118th floor, overlooking both sides of Victoria Harbour.
COCKTAIL: The Royal Kowloon Yacht Club

2 The Ocean An ocean-themed French-Japanese restaurant and bar that contributes 50 per cent of all still- and sparkling-water sales to a charity whose mission it is to clean up the world's oceans.
COCKTAIL: Sea Breeze

3 The Lobby Lounge at The InterContinental
The only hotel situated on the harbour front.
COCKTAIL: Smoke & Mirrors

4 Aqua A choice of Japanese and Italian dining waits at this super stylish bar and eatery on the 29th floor, boasting handsome harbour views.
COCKTAIL: Aqua Queen

5 Sevva You'll get a 360-degree view of the Hong Kong skyline and East meets West cocktails at this swanky operation.
COCKTAIL: Pink Sangria

Singapore

I wasn't off the plane for more than an hour before I was sitting on an emerald leather stool in the Long Bar at Raffles Hotel. No, I wasn't that desperate for a drink, but I was keen to make the most of the short stopover and a visit here was at the top of my list – many people's lists, as it turned out, the place is always packed. And they come for one thing – the Singapore Sling.

This iconic, vibrantly hued cocktail is inextricably linked with Singapore's history. There are various claims for its creation, but Raffles Hotel shouts the loudest and has the most illustrious fan base, among them Noel Coward and Somerset Maugham, so I'm not going to argue with its version of events.

Are you sitting comfortably? After the turn of the 20th century, the Long Bar at Raffles, in colonial Singapore, became the watering hole of choice for British Society. Men would down gin or whisky, while ladies were expected to be dainty so kept to fruit juices and teas. Sensing the injustice, Ngiam Tong Boon, the resident bartender, spotted a gap in the market, and in 1915 created a cocktail that masqueraded as fruit juice. It went down a storm. Today, the Long Bar mixes, muddles and pours over 1,000 Singapore Slings a day.

According to *The Savoy Cocktail Book*, the cocktail lover's bible, first published in 1930, the Sling in its simplest form is made from dissolving a teaspoon of sugar in water, adding gin and ice, and topping with soda water.

A Singapore Sling ramps things up a bit by shaking together gin, cherry brandy and lemon juice, pouring over ice and topping up with soda water. But the Singapore Sling in the Long Bar at Raffles is a decidedly more

elaborate affair. To the gin and cherry brandy you add Bénédictine, Cointreau and a dash of bitters, before finishing with pineapple, lime juice and grenadine. Not one for making on the boat, then. Pretty splendid, though.

That brings me back to boats and cocktails. We can't leave Singapore without a mention of the Republic of Singapore Yacht Club. Known as the Royal Singapore Yacht Club until 1967 (changing its name soon after independence), regattas have been held here since 1834 and the club boasts over 190 years of history.

Life at the RSYC revolves around The Mess bar. This is where bartender Roy Heng rules the roost with his Slings and Long Island Iced Teas. Heng's hot tip? Sail to Kusu Island a few kilometres from Singapore, drop anchor in one of the turquoise lagoons and hit the pristine beaches, pre-mixing your Slings before you go.

Cheat's chicken satay

Chicken satay is the most popular bar snack at the Republic of Singapore Yacht Club, the oldest yacht club in Asia, where it's downed with copious Singapore Slings (see page 106) and ice-cold beers. Satay is one of those dishes that most of Southeast Asia lays claim to. Java, though, wins the most convincing claim – it's where Muslim traders brought in Indian kebabs, which took on a more eastern feel. What is agreed is that satay always involves grilled meat skewers – it's the marinades and sauces that vary widely. Well, I've simplified the dish by stripping it back to its bare bones – there's no lemongrass or kaffir lime leaves here, but it's still spicy, and packed with peanuts.

For 8 skewers

2 chicken thighs, skinned
3 tbsp crunchy peanut
  butter
2 tbsp light soy sauce
juice of a lime or lemon
2cm piece of ginger, grated
  (lazy ginger is fine here)
½ tsp chilli flakes
olive oil, for drizzling
wooden skewers

To serve:

½ cucumber, cut into
  chunks (optional)

Method

Cut the chicken into even bite-size pieces. In a bowl, mix the peanut butter, soy sauce, lime or lemon juice, ginger and chilli flakes. Add a couple of tablespoons of water to loosen the mixture. Stir in the chicken, making sure every piece is well coated, and set aside for 20 minutes to let the flavours mingle. Preheat the grill. Thread the chicken on to skewers, drizzle over some olive oil and place on the grill pan or a baking tray covered in foil. Grill for 12–15 minutes, or until done, turning once. Serve with chunks of cucumber, if you like.

US, West Coast

A spontaneous round of applause ripples across the wide sandy beach bathed in a sultry orange glow. It's a nightly occurrence when the skies are this clear, as the sun slips down over the horizon, picking out silhouettes of surfers as they wait patiently for a crest worth riding. Where am I? California.

I had started that particular trip in the Santa Maria Valley, in an area known collectively as California's Central Coast, home to many premium winemakers. Though less well-known than their Napa and Sonoma counterparts further up the coast, the Central Coast is consistently turning out great niche wines that have a growing following, and are a tad kinder on the wallet.

The Central Coast region stretches 100-plus miles from the vineyards south of San Francisco Bay to the subtropical climate of greater Los Angeles. It includes San Luis Obispo County and its vast Paso Robles AVA, with its potent Zinfandels, and the Santa Maria Valley near Santa Barbara, with its elegant Pinot Noirs.

Just to put things into perspective, 90 per cent of all American wine is grown in California – and the planting still continues, the potential of a vineyard site determined by what lies between it and the Pacific Ocean. We're talking marine air, and often fog, which moderates the hot climate, cooling the vineyards. And it doesn't get much cooler than the Santa Maria Valley. The star grape here is Pinot Noir. The countryside is not your typical southern Californian balmy palmy climate; it's invaded by frequent cold ocean fogs, which contribute to the intensity of the fruit and the acidity in the wines. It's also worth knowing that the grapes here are mostly owned by farmers rather than wineries, making vineyard names unusually prominent on the wine labels.

A little further south is the Santa Ynez Valley, within even easier reach of Los Angeles for the wine lover. It's just a 40-minute drive from Santa Barbara over the San Marcos

Pass in the Santa Ynez Mountains. Make time, if you can, to stay overnight in Los Olivos, where you can take your pick of more than 20 tasting rooms, with Stolpman, Qupé and Andrew Murray among the highlights.

Many of the wineries have tasting rooms in Santa Barbara itself – it's the place to go for an aperitif (the Deep Sea winery has one right on Stearns Wharf). In fact, there are so many now that you can do a lengthy wine trail without ever seeing a vineyard. Visit urbanwinetrailsb.com.

Sailing into San Francisco? Then hire a car, and head to nearby Napa and Sonoma. Napa Valley has the greatest concentration of vineyards and wineries in the state, and has made its name producing the nation's most prestigious wines – not to mention the most expensive. In short, it's one of the world's three most glamorous wine regions, along with Bordeaux and Tuscany.

Napa also has the largest number of American Viticultural Areas (AVAs), among them Stag's Leap, Rutherford and Oakville. The top wines here go for silly prices, but it's worth coming to gawp at the grandiose estates and try a few of their lesser wines to get a feel for it.

Neighbouring Sonoma feels like a breath of fresh air after flash Napa – though it has its fair share of serious wines, too. It is one of California's most diverse regions, with cool coastal pockets such as Russian River for Pinot Noir, and hot spots like Dry Creek Valley for spectacular Zinfandel.

San Diego, the US craft beer capital

A quick word about the craft beer on the US West Coast. San Diego is the craft beer capital of the US – there were 65 brewing companies the last time I counted. High-flying executives have ditched their suits for the craft brewer uniform of cargo shorts and beards, to live out their hop-fuelled dreams in a rapidly expanding market. Stone Brewing leads the way, trailblazing with its never-ending roster of innovative brews and sophisticated beer-and-food matching in its on-site beer garden, which is worth the trip alone. Other craft breweries to explore include Ballast Point, Lost Abbey and Thorn Street.

Sailors have been saluting the setting sun with rum for centuries. But how rum came to be a part of sailing history is more than a coincidence – the tradition of rum and the sea began in the Caribbean.

Thankfully, rum is having a well-deserved renaissance – no hip new bar in London or New York opens without a decent rum list. And there's no better place to get acquainted with it than in its spiritual home, the Caribbean.

Does rum differ from island to island? Does where sugar cane grows make a difference? Yes, a little, but it's how rum is made that makes the real difference. We're talking pot stills versus column stills, bourbon casks versus sherry casks, and the all-important art of blending, which distillers rightly fuss over to achieve balance and elegance.

Ok, so I'm talking golden aged rum here. That said, Navy Rum is going through something of a revival – on Tortola, in the British Virgin Islands, where a Canadian ex-marine brought Pusser's Rum back to life.

Caribbean

Grenada

They call it the Spice Island. I remembered this as I downed my first rum punch in Grenada, inhaling a generous dusting of freshly grated nutmeg that was grown here. The island is relatively unspoiled, compared to the glitz of Barbados. Even the tourist hub, Grand Anse, is pretty low-key. The north of the island feels even more remote – and forget signposts, once you've left the capital, you're on your own.

As you weave your way through pastel-coloured villages, drop by the Belmont Estate to see how cocoa beans and nutmeg are picked and processed, before arriving on the choppy north-east coast and the River Antoine distillery.

While some of its neighbours in the Caribbean have struggled, the fertile island of Grenada has managed to retain a rich rum-making tradition. Here, thanks to the lush landscape – cocoa, fruits and spices all happily grow alongside the sugar cane. Grenada is a living rum museum – and the exhibits don't get much more historical than at River Antoine.

The privately owned distillery boasts an ancient water wheel, which powers the cane press, and it's worth the trip here alone. It dates back to 1785 and runs all year round. But here's the thing – the concentration of sugar in the cane is at its highest during the dry season, from January to May (in theory), while the water wheel works best during

the rainy season, from June to December. It seems to work out, though.

I love the fact that the island's only railway line takes bundles of spent sugar cane on a short trip to the tip, where it dries in the sun and becomes a fertiliser called *bagasse*, which is used back in the sugar-cane fields and to power the 'coppers' that concentrate the sugar before fermentation. I also love the fact that fermentation happens spontaneously here, letting the natural yeasts in the air do their thing once the hot juice has been spooned into the cooling tanks. The distillation is wood-fired, too.

Strictly speaking, the stuff you can buy at the distillery wouldn't be allowed on the plane home – at 140 per cent proof, it's way too flammable. But there is a plane-friendly bottling at 86 per cent proof.

The largest and best-known distillery in Grenada is Clarke's Court, located in the south of the island, in Woodlands Valley. Dutch colonists came to Grenada in the 1670s and attacked the island, seizing land, including the Woodlands Valley area, and renaming it Court Bay. The French then recaptured it, and a gentleman called Gedney Clarke made a deal and snapped up the land – hence the name Clarke's Court.

The best Clarke's Court rum is Old Grog. Apparently the name dates back to when the rum was shipped to King George III. In order to identify it as the king's rum, the casks were marked G.R.O.G. – an abbreviation for Georgius Rex Old Grenada.

I did manage to take away a recipe for a rather delicious cocktail, which you can sample after your tour – the Grenadian Kiss. Fill a tumbler with ice, add a shot of coffee liqueur (such as Tia Maria), a shot of Clarke's Court Superior Light Rum, and three shots of milk. Shake together and serve over ice.

British Virgin Islands

You haven't lived until you've downed a Painkiller at the Soggy Dollar on Jost Van Dyke – that's what Belongers will tell you. Let me translate. A Painkiller is a rum-based cocktail, the Soggy Dollar is a bar (a great bar), Jost Van Dyke is an island – one of more than 50 islands spread over 1,000 square miles in the British Virgin Islands (BVI), and a Belonger is what the islanders call themselves.

You need to be a savvy sailor to navigate the BVI. There's a brisk wind here, plus there are so many nooks and crannies to explore, and there's rum, with its strong links to naval heritage.

In 1648, a group of Dutch colonists built a fort on the west side of Tortola and grew sugar cane – until the British arrived on the scene. The islands were of strategic importance for launching attacks against the Spanish, so in 1672 the British wrested them off the Dutch settlers, and they became the British Virgin Islands.

The British continued what the Dutch had started, carving large plantations into the hillsides and planting cotton and sugar cane. Distilleries were built and molasses and rum became the islands' main products. But the plantation way of life didn't last long in the BVI. Slaves brought to work the plantations were granted their freedom and the land went with them, giving the islanders an independence and a sense of dignity unique in the British Caribbean.

There's only one distillery remaining in the BVI, but what a distillery. Callwood on Tortola is proud of its claim to be the oldest continuously running distillery in the eastern Caribbean, using a process that has changed little in its 400-year history. It offers visitors a glimpse into the way the spirit was made long before the column still, with its use of wild yeasts, long fermentations, directly fired pot stills, and the hand-bottling and hand-labelling of its white and three-year-old rums.

Tortola is also where Pusser's Rum is blended and bottled. The pusser – a corruption of the word 'purser' – was the bloke who issued a daily tot of rum to sailors on British Royal Navy ships. By 1850, the approved measure was a quarter-gill per day and for more than a hundred years Pusser's Rum was part of British naval life – until it was decided that boozing on the job wasn't a good look. The date on which the final ration was doled out – 31 July, 1970 – is known in the Navy as Black Tot Day.

It was a Canadian ex-US marine called Charles Tobias who saved the brand. He persuaded the Royal Navy to let him use the name, providing he stuck to the original recipe and donated a set amount from each case sold to the charitable Royal Navy Sailors' Fund, aka the Tot Fund. The Royal Navy agreed and the rum lives on.

Boozy tales from the BVI

'We'd been on a long delivery cruise from Houston, Texas via Florida, the Bahamas, Turks and Caicos, Dominican Republic, and Puerto Rico and we were trying to get to St Lucia by a certain date. But as often happens with boats things got in the way – storms, gear failure, the need to replace an engine, sailing directly into 30-knot trade winds, the Atlantic swell for weeks on end, not to mention threats of jail from immigration officials. The BVIs were special because we decided to stop trying to hit that deadline and enjoy a few days' holiday in the islands, sailing and exploring. That first night our skipper Ben dug a carton of 'tropical juice', some orange juice and a bottle of rum out of the lockers and mixed up something freestyle – it tasted like nectar after all that hardship. We even have a favourite bar in the BVI – Pirate's Bight on Norman Island. We pick up a mooring, mosey on over in the dinghy and land on the beach right next to the bar, listening out for the cannon fire that marks happy hour on a cocktail called Painkillers.'

Emma Bamford, author of *Casting Off* and *Untie the Lines*

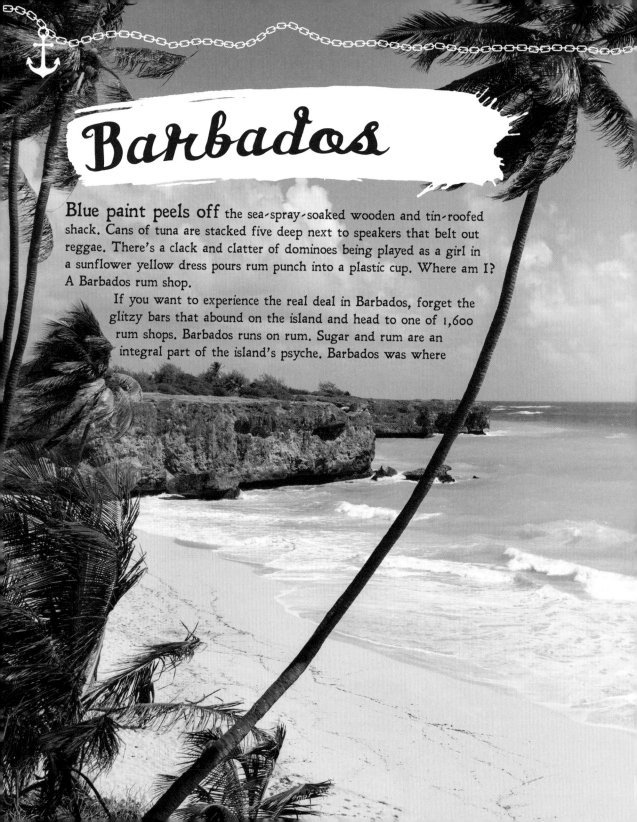

Barbados

Blue paint peels off the sea-spray-soaked wooden and tin-roofed shack. Cans of tuna are stacked five deep next to speakers that belt out reggae. There's a clack and clatter of dominoes being played as a girl in a sunflower yellow dress pours rum punch into a plastic cup. Where am I? A Barbados rum shop.

If you want to experience the real deal in Barbados, forget the glitzy bars that abound on the island and head to one of 1,600 rum shops. Barbados runs on rum. Sugar and rum are an integral part of the island's psyche. Barbados was where the English discovered that they could make their fortune in sugar; and they put rum on the map.

I first developed a taste for rum after a holiday here a decade ago – my first time in the Caribbean. We savoured 'hard cokes' (rum and coke), made with Mount Gay Extra Old at the John Moore bar in Weston, St James, where the former Barbadian PM liked to drop by; tried Old Brigand, made by Foursquare, with ginger ale at the bright-blue-and-green painted Hercules Bar at Oistins Fish Market on the south coast; and I asked

for soda water and a slice of lime with Cockspur Five Star (the island's most popular rum) at Dicia's, opposite the Post Office, a bit further down the road. For a non-alcoholic kick, I drank mauby, a fermented drink made from the bitter bark of the mauby tree.

I think Mount Gay would rather you first sampled their flagship rum without swamping it in Coke. Mount Gay is one of the big three rum producers on the island, after the West Indies Rum Distillery, home of Malibu and Cockspur, and Foursquare. A tour around its visitor centre in Bridgetown is a good introduction to the rum distilling process.

If you can, also make time for a visit to Foursquare. The taxi will bump you along potholed roads, past endless fields of sugar cane and picturesque but ramshackle villages with impeccably turned-out schoolchildren, before arriving at the Caribbean's most modern rum plant, run with passion by charismatic owner Richard Seale.

Another favourite is the recently renovated rum distillery at St Nicholas Abbey in the far north of the island, where Seale consults. Follow the long driveway lined with mahogany trees to the imposing Jacobean plantation house. The rum distillery alongside comes complete with a steam-driven mill, the last in the Caribbean, all beautifully renovated by local architect Larry Warren. The molasses cookies sold in the café are worth the trip alone.

Jerked fish skewers and chutney mayo

Picture the scene: Bridgetown fish market in Barbados, blue-welly-booted ladies expertly filleting flying fish, chattering loudly over the cries of the fish sellers. I scoffed them later in a beachside shack, squashed between a burger bun, spiced up with some Bajan seasoning. But forget trying to fillet them yourself – it takes years of practice. Any firm white fish would work well here – particularly swordfish and monkfish tail. It's a worthy substitute for the more usual jerked chicken – the bold spicing working its way deep into the meaty flesh.

For 4

500g firm white fish from
   sustainable sources
2 tsp jerk seasoning
2 tbsp rapeseed oil
salt

To serve:

thin strips of mild red
   chillies (optional)
1 lemon, cut into quarters
cocktail sticks

For the chutney mayo:

3 tbsp mayonnaise
1 tbsp mango chutney
1 tsp curry powder

Method

Trim the fish of all skin and bone and cut it into 2cm cubes. Combine the jerk seasoning and oil, rub over the fish, and leave to marinate for 30 minutes. Preheat the oven to 200°C/fan 180°C/gas 6. Combine all the mayo ingredients and set aside. Line a baking tray with foil and oil it lightly before placing the fish onto it and cook for 8 minutes. Pile the fish on a plate and scatter over the strips of red chillies, if using. Serve with the lemon wedges and the chutney mayo, for dipping.

Cocktails

Making cocktails is an art. Any good bartender will tell you that. It doesn't matter if there are only two or three ingredients – it's about balance, and getting that right is everything, whether you are at home or on board. The perfect cocktail should please the eye, excite the nose and seduce the palate. It's a balance between sweetness and sharpness, texture and colour – even if it is just a Dark & Stormy (see page 131). It's funny to think that some of the most popular cocktails we drink today were served up during Prohibition, from the Martini to the Collins (see page 135) – you're drinking history. Don't want to follow a recipe? Then use ingredients that don't fight – surely emptying the contents of your parents' drinks cabinet when you were a teenager taught you something? Don't want to drink alcohol? You won't miss the booze in my recipes (see page 160). When it comes to cocktails on board, we're talking recipes with the minimum number of ingredients – so choose your poison and stock your locker accordingly.

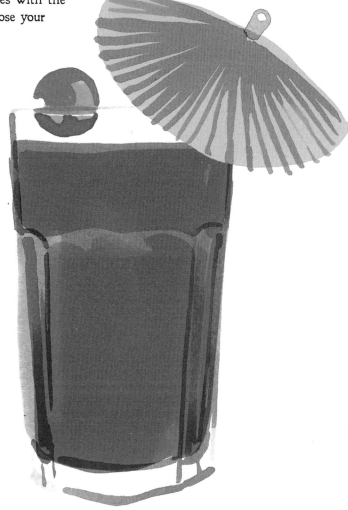

Measure for measure

When it comes to mixing cocktails, each side of the Atlantic has its own variation on the fluid ounce and the gill, with the centilitre and millilitre offering yet more systems of measurement, just to complicate matters.

But as long as all the ingredients are measured by the same means, it doesn't really matter which one you use. I favour the shot measurement on board – who wants to be fiddling around with millilitres or centilitres on the water? In the US, the shot is generally 1½oz, measured by a gadget called a jigger. But in the UK, a shot is 25ml, also measured by a jigger. So one shot in *The Boat Drinks Book* is also 25ml, two shots is 50ml. Are you keeping up?

I encourage you to buy a jigger – it's the easiest, quickest method for measuring out spirits, and measure you should. Balance, as I keep banging on, is key to a good cocktail. Where to buy a jigger? John Lewis has them, and jiggers are plentiful online, try drinkstuff.com. I favour a double jigger, with both 25ml and 50ml.

Don't have a jigger? There are other ways to make the perfect cocktail. Use a tablespoon, which holds 15ml of liquid. Two tablespoons and you have a (generous) shot. Eggcups also double up as great measuring cups.

COCKTAIL LINGO EXPLAINED

Build – To pour individual liquid ingredients directly into the glass.

Dash – A small amount.

Garnish – Ultimately a garnish should be simple, edible, and help balance the flavour of the drink.

Muddle – An old term meaning to crush with vigour, especially when using fresh herbs, such as mint. A wooden muddler lets you crush the mint without breaking the glass – about four or five times should do it.

On the rocks – Served over ice cubes.

Shake – Always shake for about 10 seconds and don't shake a fizzy drink.

Stir – Drinks made in a mixing glass need just a couple of quick stirs to combine the ingredients, more if you are using a whole jug. If you are topping up a drink with soda water, for example, a quick stir is all you need.

Twist – A thin, long strip of peel is twisted in the middle and dropped into the drink. For the perfect citrus twist: cut the rind as thinly as possible, ideally about 3½ cm long.

Rum

I fell in love with rum in Barbados. I'll never forget that first sip of rum punch – sand between my toes, sun going down, tree frogs singing. It was a good one, too – no e-number-packed lime mix (used by lots of bars in the Caribbean), but freshly squeezed limes, a dash of Angostura bitters, freshly grated nutmeg. That prompted more exploration, different cocktails (love a rum sour), graduating to sipping rums. In short, rum is my spirit of choice.

So what is rum, exactly? There are as many definitions of what constitutes rum as there are countries that make it. In a nutshell, rum is the spirit distilled from the fermented sugars derived from the fresh juice or molasses extracted from the sugar cane plant.

You can thank the Spanish and Portuguese, who brought the sugar cane plant with them to the newly discovered Caribbean islands and Brazil in the early part of the 15th century. By the end of the 17th century, the French, English and Dutch had joined in developing a taste for it – and they haven't looked back.

How is rum made?

Sugar cane grows quickly, and harvesting starts in February and continues until June or July. The canes are then cut, shredded and crushed by rollers, which separate the juice from the spent plant fibres. The juice is then cleaned and boiled, before extracting liquid from the crystals. Eventually you're left with a thick, black, sweet, gooey gunk called molasses. Yeast is added (though some distillers use native yeasts) and it's left to ferment for a period from two days to over a fortnight, before being ready to distil using either a pot or column still.

Most white and overproof rums are kept in tank for a short period before being bottled. Lighter rums spend one to two years in mostly ex-Bourbon casks, while darker, heavier rums sit for three to four years, or up to ten years or more, in barrel, to get even more flavour and colour – the rum reacts with the wood, sucking up more flavour, gradually turning the rum from clear to golden and eventually darker brown. How long it spends

8 THINGS YOU NEED TO KNOW ABOUT RUM

1 Prohibition was the beginning of a golden age of rum cocktails. Bartenders flocked to Cuba to cook up ideas, naming their drinks after famous customers such as Caruso, Dorothy Gish and Mary Pickford.

2 During Prohibition, citizens enjoyed booze shipped in by 'rum-runners', who picked up cases of rum from the West Indies and transported them to 'Rum Row' off the US coast, where they waited for the bootleggers' boats.

3 A tulip-shaped sherry copita, a brandy snifter or even a white wine glass is perfect for tasting rum – it concentrates the aromas. Look for brightness and clarity; observe the viscosity; now sniff, noting the aromas – and finally, taste.

4 Rum has always been used in mixed drinks. The early planters drank it watered down with added sugar, a sprinkling of nutmeg and often a dash of fresh fruit – cue recipes for punches, juleps, fizzes and flips.

5 Back in 1655, sailors in the British Navy used to drink rum because the water was so bad. By 1733 an official rum ration was introduced and it became part of the daily ration.

6 For most of us, rum is a Caribbean product, a sweet spirit of the laid-back lifestyle of these tropical islands, yet Latin America produces more spirit from sugar cane than anywhere else.

7 Does rum differ from place to place? Does where sugar cane grows create a specific terroir? It makes a small difference, yes, but it is how rum is made that makes them all different.

8 The oldest existing rum company in the world is Mount Gay in Barbados, dating back to 1705.

in the barrel and how many times the barrel is used both play a part in the final character.

The climate, too, has a role. Stand in the humid heat of the barrel room in a Caribbean distillery and you can fully appreciate the speedy ageing process – some say that one year of maturation in the Caribbean is equivalent to three years in a cooler climate. And yes, a certain amount evaporates from the barrel while it ages (which distillers rather sweetly call the angels' share).

The rums are then blended – each to its own recipe, some using rums from different stills, distilleries, ages, barrel types, and even countries to make up their blends. Rum is complex stuff.

Now see overleaf for *Five* **GREAT RUM** *cocktails:*

Rum punch

I make no apologies for repeating this recipe from *The Boat Cookbook*. It's the most popular drink I make. And I have LaurelAnn Morley at The Cove restaurant in Barbados to thank for it – she first sang this little ditty to me. The ratio works for any punch, pretty much. All together now: 'One of sour, two of sweet, three of strong and four of weak.' Hey presto, perfect – if rather lethal – punch.

1 shot fresh lime juice
2 shots sugar syrup
3 shots rum
4 shots water
dash or two of
   Angostura bitters

Garnish:

pinch of freshly grated
   nutmeg

Method

Stir all the ingredients together until well combined. Serve over lots of crushed ice; add a few drops of Angostura bitters and sprinkle with the grated nutmeg before serving.

Painkiller

Daphne Henderson, the founder of the Soggy Dollar bar in White Bay on the island of Jost Van Dyke in the British Virgin Islands, came up with the original of this now legendary cocktail. She wouldn't share the exact proportions, but her friend Charles Tobias, of Pusser's Rum, which is made in the BVI, came up with what he thought was a good approximation after he managed to sneak a sample back through the surf and over the gunwale of his boat. He played around with different ingredients until he got the right balance, but all credit goes to Henderson for creating the addictive concoction in the first place. But be warned – it creeps up on you.

2 shots rum
4 shots pineapple juice
1 shot orange juice
1 shot coconut cream

Garnish: freshly grated nutmeg

Method

Shake all the ingredients vigorously. Pour into a glass filled with ice and grate over the nutmeg.

Mojito

The craze for mojitos shows no sign of slowing up. It's still one of the world's most popular cocktails and it's wonderfully simple to make. Some say it dates back to the mid-16th century. In Cuba, where the mojito rules, they make this with the local *yerba buena* mint, which makes a real difference to the flavour; and in Cuba, they take care not to bruise the mint, handling it delicately. It was also said to be one of Ernest Hemingway's favourites, and he would hold court in Bar Floridita in Havana, chugging his way through glass after glass, undoubtedly popularising the drink. 'Always do sober what you said you'd do drunk,' Hemingway once wrote. Not a bad maxim to follow.

fresh mint leaves
1 tsp sugar syrup
½ lime
2 shots white or silver rum
soda water

Garnish: sprig of mint

Method

In a tall glass, muddle the mint and sugar syrup. Squeeze juice from the lime into the glass and add the lime half. Add the rum and ice. Stir. Top up with soda water. Stir again. Garnish with a sprig of mint.

Dark & Stormy

Another repeat customer from *The Boat Cookbook*, it's the mainstay of cocktail-drinking sailors everywhere. It hails from Bermuda, though the origins are rather fuzzy. What you're looking for is the perfect balance between the tangy snap of ginger beer and the richness of the rum. The addition of lime isn't authentic, but it tastes good.

2 shots dark rum
3 shots ginger beer
½ shot fresh lime juice

Method

Mix all the ingredients together in a tall glass and fill it up with ice.

Piña Colada

This has to be one of the most glamorous cocktails ever. It originated in Puerto Rico, though apparently two bartenders there claimed it as their own, one in 1954, the other in 1963. Technically you need a good blender to crush the ice but as we're on a boat I find wrapping the ice in a clean tea towel and giving it a few whacks with a rolling pin works almost as well. Be warned, don't be tempted to add ice cubes to your glass as it will melt and detract from the creaminess, killing the drink.

2 shots coconut milk
2 shots golden rum
2½ shots unsweetened pineapple juice
1-2 tbsp sugar syrup
juice of ½ lime

Garnish: pineapple wedge, maraschino cherry, cocktail umbrella (all optional)

Method

Stir the coconut milk to make sure it hasn't separated into water and cream. Then add all the ingredients into a shaker with the bashed ice and shake well. Strain into a chilled glass. If using, garnish with the pineapple wedge, cherry and cocktail brolly.

Gin

Not so long ago, ordering a G&T was a simple affair – a measure of Gordon's, a splosh of mainstream mixer and a slice of lemon. Wind forward to the present day and you'll be asked what brand of gin you prefer, with the barman pointing proudly at his line-up of boutique gins crowding his back bar, and he'll ask you which tonic water you would like, from a new generation headed up by Fever-Tree. And you might get a twist of cucumber instead of lemon – or rhubarb, or even grapefruit. Gin is experiencing the kind of boom that the wine industry went through in the 1980s.

There are now more than 500 brands of gin, from Spain and Germany to France and the US. The biggest exporter, though, is the UK. Gin's revival can be traced back to the early Noughties, when Scottish whisky firm William Grant & Sons launched lighter, more floral-tasting Hendrick's at a higher price point – it took off. It was followed by a wave of boutique distillers, most notably Sipsmith in London.

We have the Dutch to thank for gin. After monks brought immune-system-boosting juniper-based elixirs into Europe at the time of the Black Death, the Dutch ran with it, refining the distillation – soon everyone was drinking it, and not just as a health tonic.

Genever, as the Dutch call it, was handed out to English mercenaries who were helping out the Dutch in the Thirty Years' War. They brought home tales of 'Dutch Courage' and no doubt a few bottles, too. Gin, as the English now called it, became fashionable, and within a few years our cities were awash with it – by 1730, a fifth of London's houses were gin shops.

Navy Strength Gin

The Isle of Wight Distillery has linked up with the National Museum of the Royal Navy in Portsmouth to produce HMS Victory Navy Strength Gin. The enterprise also includes a limited edition oak-aged Navy Strength Gin using a barrel made from the actual oak from HMS *Victory*. Launched on 7 May, 1765, the legendary ship was instrumental in winning Britain's greatest naval victory, the Battle of Trafalgar, under Vice-Admiral Nelson. In the days before rum, all naval ships had to carry gin on board. It was stored in barrels in the hold next to the gunpowder and the concern was that if the barrels leaked and made the gunpowder damp, it would leave the ship without firepower. However, alcohol with a strength of 57 per cent plus would still ignite. So the purser would carry out a test before the barrels of gin were rolled on to the ship, by taking a small amount of gunpowder and soaking it in gin before igniting. If the gunpowder ignited they carried on loading up the ship – if not, the barrels were returned, as the gin was less than 57 per cent.

How is gin made?

Gin is both simple and complex. First alcohol is distilled from something – in the case of most high-end gins it's grain, such as wheat. But it's the next distillation that makes good gin what it is.

Cue the botanicals, which vary widely from coriander and cardamom to citrus peel and cinnamon, and, of course, juniper, which looks like peppercorns and grows on pine-like scrubby bushes, mainly in Italy. The only rule is that the finished gin must taste predominantly of juniper.

This and other botanicals are added to the neutral alcohol, which is distilled again to infuse the spirit with flavour, with actual berries, flowers, petals and spices floating around in the still (it's more like cooking than making any other spirit). Then it's cut with pure water to bring down the alcohol levels to a drinkable proof.

Gin styles explained

There are four main styles of gin, Dutch Genever, Old Tom, Compound Gin and London Dry. London Dry is what most of us think of as gin. But get this – London Dry does not have to be made in London. Instead it's defined by getting its juniper flavour from a neutral spirit (such as grain alcohol), redistilled with botanicals, with nothing added after the redistillation process. Some gins do add flavour after redistillation, most famously Hendrick's, which adds cucumber – not that there's anything wrong with that, it just can't be called a London Dry.

8 THINGS YOU NEED TO KNOW ABOUT GIN

1 In 1726, London had 1,500 working stills and 6,287 places where you could buy gin.

2 Gin and gingerbread, anyone? This was the first known pairing in 1731. When the Thames froze over, a glass of hot gin and a slice of gingerbread was the favourite street food of the day.

3 How to taste gin: dilute with an equal measure of water and serve at room temperature – it shows up both its qualities and flaws.

4 Gin and tonic is huge in Spain, where they call it 'gin tonic'. Served in balloon wine glasses and garnished with all manner of unusual botanicals, the craze started in Michelin-starred restaurants in the north of the country. Other big gin-drinking nations are the Philippines, who drink more than anyone else, the United States, and of course, the UK.

5 The gin of old was pretty rough stuff, often spiked with unsavoury ingredients like turpentine, and necked by the pint by cash-poor Brits desperate to get 'Drunk for a penny, dead drunk for twopence', as the grog shop signs proudly announced.

6 The gin and tonic – or G&T, as everyone calls it – first came to fame in the British colonies as the quinine in tonic water was found to be an effective deterrent against malaria. As quinine was a tad bitter in its raw state, gin was added to make it more palatable.

7 Gin has a history of being used 'for medicinal purposes'. The Royal Navy mixed gin with lime cordial to ward off scurvy, while the quinine in tonic was their go-to malaria prophylactic.

8 Nearly all juniper used in gin is picked wild.

Five **GREAT GIN** cocktails:

Collins

I love a Collins. So refreshing, so simple, and you can still clearly taste the gin (a good thing). The original Collins cocktail was called a John Collins, named after a waiter working at a hotel and coffee house in London at the end of the 18th century. His original version used a Dutch-style gin, soda, lemon and sugar. A few decades later, the Americans discovered the drink and it took off – it was de rigueur during Prohibition. Today, if you are served a Collins made with bourbon or whisky, then it's called a John Collins. The story goes (and there are many versions around) that when a bartender used Old Tom gin, which is a London gin with a sweet flavour, the Collins became known as a Tom Collins. These days', bartenders serve a Collins with a London Dry gin.

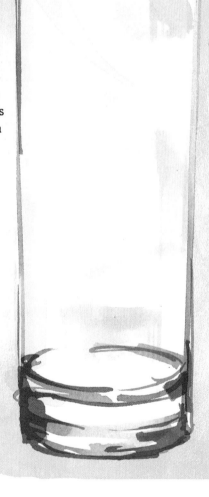

2 shots gin
1 shot freshly squeezed
   lemon juice
½ shot sugar syrup
soda water

Garnish: slice of lemon

Method

Add the first three ingredients to a tall glass and stir. Add ice and top up with soda water. Garnish with a slice of lemon dropped into the drink.

Negroni

I should really build up to the Negroni. This iconic cocktail will put hairs on your chest, but I'm going right in. To be honest, it's a bit of a Marmite drink – you either love it or hate it – but it has many fans, including a fair few chefs that I know (and me). The aromatic Martini Rosso tempers Campari's medicinal character, while the gin adds an elegant depth. Orson Welles was a fan: 'The bitters are excellent for your liver, the gin is bad for you. They balance each other,' he allegedly said of the drink. And like many of the cocktails listed on these pages, you are drinking a bit of history. The Negroni was created in 1919 by Fosco Scarselli at Caffè Cassoni in Florence for a customer called Count Camillo Negroni, who walked in one day asking for an Americano 'with a bit more kick'. He's not wrong there.

1 shot London Dry gin
1 shot Campari
1 shot sweet red Vermouth, such as
   Martini Rosso

Garnish: twist of orange peel

Method

Pour all the ingredients into a glass filled with ice and stir. Garnish with a twist of orange peel.

Pink Lady

With its light blush, thanks to the grenadine, this is a big girl's blouse of a drink. In fact, it was a favourite of high society ladies in the 1930s. The key to this drink (and any shaken with egg) is to shake it for longer than you would most cocktails. And you gotta love a drink with a pink foamy top.

2 shots gin
1 fresh raw egg white
½ shot grenadine

Garnish: twist of lemon peel

Method

Shake all the ingredients with ice and strain into a cocktail glass. Add a twist of lemon peel.

Silver Bullet

If I had to choose a desert island cocktail, then this would be it. Not for actual drinking on a desert island, you understand – that would be a rum punch. No, a Silver Bullet is my favourite drink for sipping before a smart supper at home, or out, and lately on board, too. Who cares if I follow this brilliantly simple but elegant cocktail, invented sometime in the 1920s, with sardines on toast? And I have London restaurant and bar Hawksmoor to thank for introducing me to it. The Hawksmoor group, co-created by Will Beckett, takes its cocktails very seriously, bringing back classic cocktails and inventing delicious new ones. Kummel is a famous aniseed-and-caraway-flavoured liqueur with a honeyed finish that dates back decades – I get mine from thewhiskyexchange.com.

2 shots gin
½ shot kummel
1 shot freshly squeezed lemon juice

Garnish: twist of lemon peel

Method

Shake all the ingredients with ice and strain into a chilled glass. Garnish with a twist of lemon peel.

Gin Gin Mule

This clever cocktail was created by New York mixologist Audrey Saunders. She is the founder of the Pegu Club, voted one of the top 20 bars in the world by *Forbes* magazine, and, well, she's a total star. This is my simplified version.

2 thumbnail slices of
   fresh root ginger
2 shots London Dry gin
½ shot freshly squeezed
   lime juice
¼ shot sugar syrup
6 fresh mint leaves
good-quality ginger beer

Garnish:
lime wedge

Method
Muddle the ginger in the base of a tall glass filled with ice. Add the next four ingredients. Top up with ginger beer, stir, and garnish with a lime wedge.

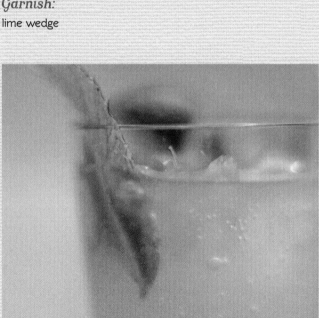

Whisky

After a cold day on the water (or a struggle to get around a headland if you're Sir Robin Knox-Johnston, see below), is there anything better than a warming glass of whisky? Though these days, pretty much any time is whisky time, whether it's enjoyed at home after dinner, in the local pub, or shaken into a sour in a smart hotel cocktail bar.

The history bit

Nobody knows who made the first whisky. What is agreed is that distillation arrived in Scotland with the monks of the Celtic Church. Back then (we're talking 6th and 7th centuries reputedly), whisky used mainly for medicinal purposes. It was laced with heather, honey, herbs and spices – think whisky liqueur. And it pretty much stayed that way right up until the beginning of the 19th century. It was only when the grand families and crofters alike got in on the act that it began to taste more like it does today.

Distillers have always used the main crop of their region as the base for their spirits, and in Scotland that meant barley. Making whisky was seen as a great way to use up surplus grain. It meant that cattle could be fed on the grains left after mashing and crofters could use their whisky as part-payment for their rent. Whisky soon became an integral part of rural life.

Whisky's increasing popularity attracted the attention of the Scottish Parliament, which introduced the first taxes on malt and whisky in the 17th century driving distillers underground. By the 1820s more than half the whisky consumed in Scotland was enjoyed without paying any duty. This flouting of the rules prompted a change in the law and in 1823 the Excise Act was passed sanctioning the distilling of whisky and smuggling died out.

Sir Robin Knox-Johnston's headland policy

'When all parties within a crew vote that a headland has been passed, an alcoholic beverage may be taken. It started in the two-handed Round Britain Race when the boat was embayed and would not tack. Eventually running out of space we wore her round, just avoiding the rocks, and agreed that when we passed the headland at the edge of the bay we would have a whisky.'

By 1825, the whisky industry had been building up a reputation internationally and it was now being controlled by large companies. New legislation prompted a flurry of new distilleries across the Highlands.

Cue the continuous still. In 1827, Robert Stein discovered a way to make a lighter, grain-based whisky that could be mass-produced. Later adapted by Aeneas Coffey, the continuous (or column) still changed whisky production for ever. Distillers in the Scottish Lowlands jumped on the invention; wine merchants and grocers such as John Walker, James Chivas and Matthew Gloag began blending malt with the lighter grain whisky and their customers loved it.

And it was all looking pretty good in Scotland – until the 1970s. Younger drinkers turned away from the brown stuff in favour of the white stuff – *vodka et al* – and the global whisky industry fell into a deep funk.

Fast-forward to today, and Scotch is back in favour – more than that, it's the envy of the world. There are over 130 distilleries in operation in Scotland and plenty of new openings in the offing. Not a trendy new bar opens without a decent listing, with renewed interest in how they are made and who makes them. People are drinking less, but they are drinking smarter and they're willing to pay for it. *Sláinte*!

How is malt whisky made?

It's produced from three ingredients: malted barley, water and yeast. The barley is germinated, dried over a fire, ground, mixed with hot water, fermented and then distilled twice in pot stills. The spirit is then aged in oak casks for a minimum of three years. That's it – in theory. Of course, they taste different, and that's the magic of malt. Plus, every aspect of production is subtly different in each distillery, from the type of grain used to the shape of the stills, even where it's made.

WHISKEY WITH AN 'E'

Up until fairly recently, if you were a serious whisky drinker then you would reach for Scotch. Irish whiskey was for drowning sorrows, and coffee. But things have changed, and changed fast.

Ten years ago there was no craft industry to speak of; now, there are a reported 28 new whiskey distilleries in Ireland, either proposed or underway. In short, Irish whiskey is having a moment – about time, too, as Irish whiskey once ruled the roost. Dismissive of the new blends coming out of Scotland, the Irish stuck to their guns with their pot stills. Their prestige grew, they gained a reputation internationally, especially in America, and Irish whiskey started to sell more than Scotch. At its height, in the mid-19th century, there were 88 distilleries in Ireland. Some historians claim the Irish (and many American) distillers added the 'e' to 'whisky' to distinguish themselves from the substandard Scotch that was flooding the market at the time.

But then along came Prohibition and the bootleggers. Thanks to bad counterfeits, Irish whiskey's reputation was ruined practically overnight. Then came the ban of Irish products in Britain and the Empire, and the Irish whiskey industry imploded.

Today, three companies produce most of the Irish whiskey available, but the rest comes from newcomers such as Dublin's Teeling Distillery. There's a new optimism in Ireland right now, which is good news for whiskey lovers.

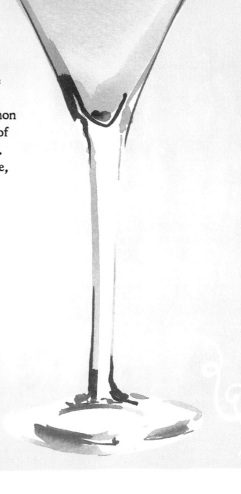

Five GREAT WHISKY cocktails:

Apple Mac

Scotch, ginger and apple is an utterly
brilliant combination, but not one I can take
credit for, sadly. The Apple Mac, a riff on
the classic Whisky Mac, was created by Simon
Difford, founder of diffordsguide.com, one of
the largest and most visited drinks websites.
You'll find all your cocktail recipe needs here,
but if you would rather read something in
print, Difford has published several drinks
books, with *Difford's Guide to Cocktails*
the best known.

2 shots Scotch
1½ shots pressed apple juice
½ shot Stone's Original Green Ginger Wine

Garnish: apple slice (optional)

Method

Shake all the ingredients with ice and strain
into a chilled glass. Garnish with an apple slice,
if using.

Rob Roy

Created at the Waldorf Astoria in New York to celebrate the 1894 premiere of the operetta *Rob Roy*, which celebrated a Scottish rebel hero, this is basically a Manhattan made with Scotch. And as with the Manhattan there are various permutations, but I like this one, served on the rocks.

1 shot whisky
1 shot sweet vermouth
1 or 2 dashes Angostura bitters

Garnish: twist of orange

Method

Combine the ingredients in a mixing glass (you can use the shaker) filled with ice and stir. Strain into a chilled cocktail glass and drop in a twist of orange to give it extra zest.

Whisky sour

The trick to getting a sour just right is balancing the sugar and lemon to achieve that perfect lip-puckering kick. It's more usual to include American rye whiskey, such as Jim Beam, or bourbon in a whiskey sour (note the addition of the 'e' – for more detail see page 142), but if they aren't a regular in your boat locker, you can happily substitute it with blended Scotch whisky.

2 shots blended whisky
½ shot lemon juice
½ shot sugar syrup

Method

Shake all the ingredients with ice and strain into a glass.

Whisky Smash

A smash is one of the most refreshing cocktails out there. Though on board you'll have to take your rolling pin to the ice. First created back in the 19th century, smashes are popular once more. You can use Scotch, sure, but I actually prefer this one with a rye whiskey, such as Jim Beam.

7 fresh mint leaves
½ lemon, quartered lengthways
1 tbsp sugar syrup
2 shots rye whiskey

Garnish: mint sprigs

Method

Using a muddler (or the handle of a wooden spoon), mash the mint leaves, lemon quarters, and sugar syrup in a mixing glass or cocktail shaker 4–5 times to release the juices and oils. Add the whiskey. Strain into a tumbler half-filled with crushed ice. Stir, then pile in more crushed ice. Garnish with a sprig of mint.

The Walking Earl

I came across this concoction recently by way of Henrietta Lovell, founder of the Rare Tea Company. Lovell is aiming to bring back and reinvent an age-old combination that ruled in London in the 16th century – punch made from tea, lemon, sugar and brandy. Tea was the perfect mixer and far safer than water back in the day, and it provided the bitter element that is key to the well-balanced cocktail. Now all the top bartenders are using tea in their cocktails – so why not boaters, too? It's a cup of tea on holiday. Umbrella optional.

3 tsp Earl Grey tea
   leaves
1 shot whisky
1 tsp clear honey,
   or to taste

Garnish:
twist of orange

Method

Infuse the tea leaves in 500ml of cold water for an hour, keeping it chilled if possible. Strain the tea infusion, then mix 100ml of it with a shot of whisky in a cocktail shaker, and sweeten with the honey, shaking until it dissolves. Pour into an ice-filled glass and garnish with a twist of orange.

Vodka

Of all the spirits, vodka used to baffle me the most. If I drank it at all, it was in a Bloody Mary, or as part of a dry Martini. Baffling because it appeared to lack character, just a means of getting people drunk. But after digging a little deeper I found differences in texture, viscosity and flavour between the brands – vodka is more diverse than you might think.

So who made it first? It's difficult to sum up vodka's history in one neat little paragraph because it has evolved differently in each of the countries where it is the national spirit. And in case you are thinking 'Vodka is just vodka, right?', in Poland, Russia and Scandinavia it's much more than that – it's a social event with its own rituals.

Poland is probably the best place to start, as there is convincing evidence that peasants in the 8th century were making a crude alcoholic spirit by freezing wine, though the first written record of making a spirit from grain comes in 1405, pre-dating Russia's efforts with the spirit.

As in every other country, these early spirits were initially used as medicines and spiced up with infusions of herbs, spices, roots and sugar – so not the neat, clear spirit we know today. By the end of the 16th century, Poland was producing enough vodka to start exporting. With the arrival of triple distillation and charcoal filtering in the 18th century, a new stronger, cleaner style of vodka was born, becoming the model for quality production across Eastern Europe.

If Poland lays claim to being the first vodka producer, then its image is still associated with Russia. The spirit doesn't freeze in Russia's harsh winters, thanks to its high alcohol content – which has taken it from keeping moods buoyant in desperate times to being the darling of the new bourgeoisie that it still is today.

The West, meanwhile, took a little longer to discover vodka. We've made up for it now, though, with inventive vodka-based cocktails, and a line-up of quality sipping vodkas available in a smart bar near you.

How is vodka made?

Technically speaking, vodka is pure (usually rectified) spirit that has been distilled with water and filtered before bottling. The aim of the game is to achieve the purest spirit possible.

Neutral spirit can be made from anything that contains starch – in theory, vodka can be

6 THINGS YOU NEED TO KNOW ABOUT VODKA

1 Did James Bond get it right? Should a vodka Martini be shaken or stirred? Shaking aerates, stirring dilutes. Which is better? You decide. Though some find that shaking can add a pleasing lightness – just saying.

2 Pasta and vodka? Believe it. Vodka pasta is a classic dish that dates back to the 1970s Italian-American kitchen. There are numerous versions, some adding chilli, others bacon, but all involve garlic, tomatoes, cream and pasta – Nigella adds her vodka straight on to the drained pasta.

3 A litre of vodka weighs only 953g and not 1kg as you might think – vodka is less dense than water.

4 You might have heard the term 'the Vodka Belt' – it refers to the countries that make and drink vodka, from Russia, Ukraine and Belarus, all Nordic and Baltic countries, to Poland and some areas of Slovakia and Hungary. *Nazdarovya!*

5 Apart from being able to make you (very, very) drunk, vodka can be used for a range of other purposes, from soaking your razor blade to disinfect and prevent rusting, to cleaning your glasses – and sailors, it can also be used for disinfecting and alleviating the pain of a jellyfish sting.

6 In Eastern Europe, vodka is usually drunk neat and ice-cold – in iced glasses.

made from ingredients such as sugar, beet, potatoes, rye, wheat, millet, maize and even whey. Most basic commercial brands, though, use molasses.

Premium vodkas are looking for finer qualities in their raw materials, and the best are made from either grain or potatoes. Rye and wheat rule in Russia, rye and potatoes in Poland, and wheat in Sweden – so already you are looking at different styles. What does each bring? Rye gives bite and weight, wheat a delicacy, while potato gives a distinct creaminess.

Water is key to any spirit and vodka is no exception – it's used twice, once for mashing and again when the spirit is diluted before filtration. Purity is achieved by a highly controlled distillation process. To get to that stage of sought-after cleanliness, vodka will be distilled two, three, four or more times.

While some vodkas are produced in pot stills, most are made in continuous or column stills, with the differences between the vodkas marked by the way in which they are rectified and later filtered. Filtration removes the spirit's raw, aggressive edge and replaces it with a mild, mellow, often sweet taste, the exact method a closely guarded secret.

And you thought vodka was a simple product?

Five GREAT VODKA cocktails:

Vodka Gimlet

Can't get hold of any fresh limes? Then this is the cocktail for you. You might have noticed that there's a theme going on here – lots of lime-based cocktails. I hold my hands up – I love them. And lime is traditionally associated with sailors, right? Lime juice was used on the high seas to combat scurvy. Though these days it's a route to a great cocktail. But sometimes you just can't get hold of any, so I suggest stashing a bottle of lime cordial in your locker. In fact, top bartenders will tell you that any kind of gimlet should be made with lime cordial – and Rose's Lime Cordial, at that, the world's first concentrated bottled fruit juice drink, dating back to 1867. What's a gimlet? When beers and spirits were stored in barrels, bartenders used a small, sharp hand tool called a gimlet to tap into them, which somewhere along the line gave its name to this little zesty cocktail. Originally made with gin and dating back to the 1930s, the vodka-based gimlet has now become more the norm.

2 shots vodka
1 shot lime cordial

Garnish: wedge of lime (optional)

Method

Combine the ingredients in a tumbler filled with ice and stir. Garnish with a lime wedge if you have one.

Moscow Mule

Back in the 1940s, two restaurateurs, John Martin from New York and Jack Morgan from Hollywood, combined their surplus of ginger beer and slow-moving Smirnoff vodka with a splash of lime to come up with the Moscow Mule. Thanks to the mule, Smirnoff's sales soared, putting vodka on America's map. It should be on every sailor's map, too – think of all those easy vodka cocktail recipes out there.

2 shots vodka
ginger beer
big wedge of lime

Method

Pour the vodka over ice cubes in a tall glass. Top up with ginger beer and squeeze over the lime juice, dropping the shell into the glass.

Salty Dog

While we're on the subject of nautical-themed cocktails, I give you the Salty Dog. It's basically a Sea Breeze without the cranberry juice, and a salty rim on the glass, a close relation to the Greyhound. It can be made with gin, too. I prefer pink grapefruit juice, as it's easier on the palate – but your call. Instead of rimming your glass in salt, you could add a pinch of sea salt to the drink to give it a pop of flavour.

wedge of lemon
pinch of coarse sea salt (Maldon is best)
2 shots vodka
3 shots grapefruit juice

Method

Rub a wedge of lemon around the rim of your glass and dip it into a saucer of coarse sea salt. Add ice and the vodka and grapefruit juice and stir.

Bloody Mary

There are many versions of this famous cocktail, which dates back to the 1920s and started (and continues) life as a hangover cure. But all we really care about is that it is one of the great restorative drinks, with enough alcohol and burst of savouriness to bring you back to life without having to face a fry-up. There are variations, of course, but all agree it should contain vodka, tomato juice and Worcestershire sauce – though I've done away with the annoying celery sticks, which just get in the way. And there is a rather brilliant spin on the Bloody Mary supposedly created for crooner Tony Bennett while he was singing at Caesar's Palace in Las Vegas, which substitutes Clamato juice for tomato, called a Bloody Caesar.

2 shots vodka
4 shots tomato juice
½ shot freshly
    squeezed lemon juice
2 dashes Worcestershire
    sauce
2 dashes Tabasco hot
    pepper sauce
pinch of celery salt
grind of black pepper

Garnish: wedge of lime

Method

Add the ingredients to a cocktail shaker or mixing glass and stir. Pour into an ice-filled glass. Garnish with a wedge of lime.

Sea Breeze

Well, I couldn't not include a cocktail called Sea Breeze in *The Boat Drinks Book*, now could I? One of the most famous vodka-based cocktails, the Sea Breeze actually started out life as something completely different, according to legendary bartender Salvatore Calabrese in his *Classic Summer Cocktails*. Back in the 1930s a Sea Breeze was made of gin, apricot brandy, grenadine and lemon juice. Later recipes featured vodka, dry vermouth, Galliano and Blue Curaçao. Quite how it morphed into the much-loved drink we know today is a mystery but I'm happy it did. Take away the grapefruit juice and you've got US East Coast classic, the **Cape Codder**.

2 shots vodka
3 shots grapefruit juice
1 shot cranberry juice

Garnish:
wedge of lime

Method
Fill a tall glass with ice cubes. Add all the ingredients and stir. Garnish with a lime wedge.

Tequila

I couldn't touch tequila for years after a misguided over-indulgence (I blame the 'slammer' girls, not myself, of course). Then I had a Margarita in Mexico. Blue skies, palm trees and a blast of warm air greeted us as we touched down in tropical Mérida, the state capital of Yucatán.

The food here has a unique style, influenced hugely by the local Mayan culture, but also by the Caribbean, Europe and even the Middle East (think spice routes). The regional specialities are some of Mexico's most unusual, from pork cooked in banana leaves (*cochinita pibil*) made with Yucatán's beloved *achiote* seasoning, to the egg-stuffed, pumpkin-seed-sauced *papadzules*.

To wash it down, we drank Margaritas. Not the frozen, slushy kind, brimming with crushed ice, but straight up, tinkling with fat ice cubes, a perfect foil for the fiery *habanero* chillies that lace many of the dishes here. And I still enjoy a Margarita, the most celebrated of all tequila cocktails – a superlative combination of *blanco* or *reposado* tequila, orange-flavoured liqueur and lime juice.

The origin of the Margarita is not clear – there are several contenders all claiming to have invented it, the oldest of which dates back to 1936, to the Crespo Hotel in Puebla. Though Tijuana also lays claim to the birth of the cocktail, as does a bar in Ciudad Juárez. It may not even have been created in Mexico at all, but in Los Angeles. But who cares, really? What's important is that we've got it, in all its forms, and it's how most of us enjoy tequila.

So what is tequila?

Ok, so here's the first thing you should know – tequila is not made from cactus, as is commonly believed. It's distilled from the heart of the blue-leaved agave, a large succulent plant that takes nearly a decade to mature in the heat of Mexico.

Tequila is Mexico. It's as integral to Mexican culture as whisky is to Scotland. The Aztecs are thought to have produced alcoholic drinks from agave as early as the 3rd century BC, with distillation dating from the 16th century. And while un-aged tequila offers fresh, earthy, herbaceous characteristics, barrel-aged varieties have a complexity to rival Cognac or malt whisky and can be enjoyed all on their lonesome.

To qualify as tequila, the blue agave must be grown in one of five designated regions – the whole of Jalisco, parts of Nayarit, Michoacán, Guanajuato and Tamaulipas, located in the Sierre Madre, the high, dry, mineral-rich plain to the north-west of Guadalajara.

You thought it had a worm in it? That's mezcal. And no, it doesn't make you hallucinate, that's just a myth. Like tequila, mezcal is made from agave. In fact, technically speaking tequila is a mezcal from a designated area. But while tequila can be made only from blue agave, mezcal can be produced from a range of different strains of agave.

The production process of mezcal is a bit different, too. It doesn't have the refinement of tequila, bar a few hand-crafted versions, and is yet to be taken seriously, thanks to the worm. The *gusano* worm, which some brands add in the bottle, is purely a marketing ploy – sorry to disappoint.

How is tequila made?

After waiting eight to ten years for the blue agave plant to reach maturity, the leaves are cut away to expose the central core, called the *piña* (pineapple). Once in the distillery, the *piñas* are cooked to convert the starches to sugar, which are then crushed and the juice drained off. The liquid is then put into large fermenting vats. It's at this point that different producers do their own thing. Some add their own strain of yeasts; others add sugar, though traditionalists rely on wild yeasts to trigger the ferment. But all tequila is double distilled in either copper or stainless-steel pot stills, most distilling to a high strength before diluting straight after. An increasing number of producers are ageing their tequilas in wood for between two and 11 months (*reposado*), and others for one year or more (*anejo*), and these make great 'sipping' tequilas.

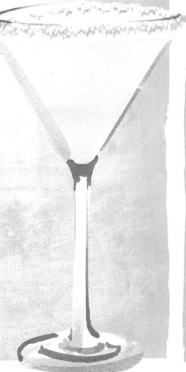

Five GREAT TEQUILA cocktails:

The Margarita

In theory, there is nothing to making a Margarita. It's not meant to blow your socks off — it's about balance, like all cocktails. It's important to use good tequila, made from 100 per cent blue agave — but don't waste a good aged tequila, which should be sipped on its own. Cointreau is the best orange-flavoured liqueur to use in a Margarita, and always use fresh limes. The best Margaritas are either shaken, or stirred on the rocks.

2 shots tequila
1 shot Cointreau
2 shots fresh
   lime juice

Garnish: salt, for
   rimming the glass

Method
Shake all the ingredients with ice and strain into a salt-rimmed glass.

Mayan Mule

Mexico's answer to the 1940s classic cocktail, the Moscow Mule. It works well, too.

2 shots tequila
squeeze of lime juice
2 dashes Angostura bitters
ginger beer

Garnish: mint sprigs, slice
   of lime (optional)

Method
Place two or three ice cubes in a glass. Pour over the tequila then add the other ingredients. Stir and garnish with a mint sprig and slice of lime, if using.

The Paloma

We tend to associate Mexico with one drink, and one drink only – the Margarita. But the country's best-loved tipple is the Paloma. Refreshing and simple, in Mexico they make it with a grapefruit-flavoured fizzy drink, but I prefer to top it up with soda. Be warned: it slips down worryingly easily.

2 shots tequila
2 shots pink grapefruit juice
1 shot fresh lime juice
½ shot sugar syrup
pinch of salt
soda water

Garnish: slice of lime (optional)

Method

Fill a glass with ice. Add all the ingredients except the soda water. Stir, top up with soda water and garnish with a slice of lime, if using.

Tequila Sunrise

The Rolling Stones got through their 1972 American tour fuelled by these, or so the story goes. And The Eagles named a song after it. Reason enough to make one, don't you think?

1 lime
2 shots tequila
4 shots orange juice
dash or two of
    grenadine

Method

Fill a tall glass with ice. Squeeze over the lime juice and drop the shell into the glass. Add the tequila then carefully pour over the orange juice. DO NOT STIR. Add the grenadine – it should sink to the bottom of the glass, creating the sunrise effect.

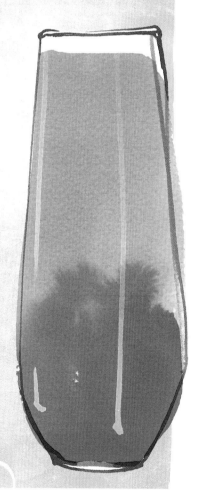

Veracruzana

This summery cocktail pays homage to Mexico's oldest port and home to the sweet Veracruz pineapple. Carmen Miranda would have approved. Don't be tempted to try this with tinned pineapple.

4 fresh 2–3cm pineapple
   chunks
2 basil leaves
2 shots tequila
1 shot sugar syrup
1 shot fresh lime juice

Garnish:

slice of fresh pineapple and
   a basil leaf (optional)

Method

Muddle the pineapple and basil leaves in a shaker. Add the remaining ingredients and some ice, and shake. Strain into a glass filled with fresh ice. Garnish with a slice of pineapple and a basil leaf, if using.

Non~alcoholic cocktails

Going 'virgin' is the new black, didn't you know? As the world becomes more health~conscious and teetotalism is on the rise (according to the National Statistics for Adult Drinking Habits), bartenders are focusing their talents on non~alcoholic drinks. They want their 'virgin' cocktails to taste as good as their boozy counterparts, and they are going to great lengths to achieve that, from installing clever bits of kit, such as the £10k rotary evaporator, to using pipette jars of acids to add balance in place of alcohol. Cue a raft of savoury, vegetable~ and tea~based cocktails in top bars around town. Yup, welcome to the era of creative non~alcoholic drinks. Ok, so you need to scale things back somewhat for the boat but you can learn a thing or two from these clever bar folk − if only that staying sober is seriously chic.

Five GREAT NON-ALCOHOLIC cocktails:

Gunner

This is the non-alcoholic cocktail *du jour* at the Royal Hong Kong Yacht Club – and now my top booze-free tipple on board. Little tip: buy good-quality ginger ale and beer – the Fever-Tree brand is a favourite – and measure equal parts of each. If you're stuck for fresh limes, use a splosh of lime cordial.

150ml ginger ale
½ lime
1–2 dashes Angostura bitters
150ml ginger beer

Garnish: sprig of mint (optional)

Method

Add ice to your glass. Add the ginger ale followed by the lime, cut into quarters, squeezed and dropped in, and then the bitters. Top up with the ginger beer and stir. Serve garnished with a sprig of mint, if using.

Apple and Elderflower Spritz

So summery, so English, so quaffable – so I've gone for a large jug of it, my twist on a Mockito. Makes about 10 drinks.

juice of 2 limes
1 litre apple juice
500ml sparkling water
125ml elderflower cordial

Garnish: mint sprigs

Method

In a large jug, mix the lime juice with the apple juice, sparkling water and elderflower cordial. Stir and serve over ice with a sprig of mint.

Shirley Temple

This is an old one – but a good one. Allegedly created for the child star back in the 1930s by a Beverly Hills bartender.

½ shot grenadine
½ shot freshly squeezed lime juice
200ml ginger ale

Garnish: maraschino cherry (optional)

Method

Fill a glass with ice cubes, add the grenadine and lime juice, top with the ginger ale, stir and then garnish with a cocktail cherry, if using.

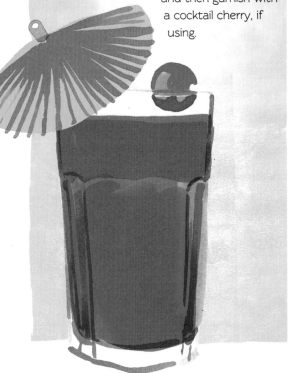

Sangrita

Talk about waking up your senses – this traditional drink from Mexico will get the party started without a drop of alcohol. Makes about 10 drinks.

1 litre tomato juice
500ml orange juice
5 tsp clear honey
juice of 3 limes
pinch of salt
1 red chilli, finely chopped
1 tbsp finely chopped white onion
20 drops Worcestershire sauce

Method

Put all the ingredients into a jug and stir well, making sure the honey is dissolved. Pour straight from the jug into ice-filled tumblers.

Cucumber Smash

This always reminds me of the summer I once spent in Turkey, buying cold cucumbers from sellers on the beach – cucumber never tasted so good.

½ cucumber
2cm piece of root
  ginger, grated
500ml apple juice
½ lime

Garnish:

strips of cucumber

Method

Grate the cucumber into a bowl. Stir in the ginger and the apple juice and squeeze over the lime. Strain the mixture into a jug and pour into ice-filled tumblers. Finish with strips of cucumber, if you fancy.

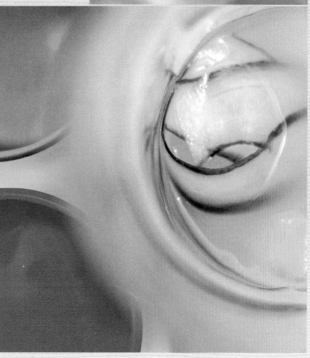

How beer is made

As grapes are to wine, barley is to beer. Or I should say malted barley. Beer is brewed mainly from malted barley, hops, yeast and water. Not just hops, as most people think. Hops are used much like spice, and hop cones contain a wealth of resins and essential oils, which give beer its distinctive bitterness and hop flavour. And brewers don't use any old barley – there are selected varieties, like Maris Otter, that are particularly suited to being malted. Thanks to our maritime climate, British malt is among the best in the world.

Other sources of fermentable carbohydrate can be used, of course, such as maize, wheat and rice, plus other natural ingredients, to create different styles and flavours.

A quick word about yeast. Brewers use specially selected yeasts to produce distinctive flavours in their beers. Not that they'll tell you which, exactly – it's a closely guarded secret.

There are over 100 different styles of beer in a dizzying range of flavours, from pilsners to pale ales, stouts to bocks.

Ten steps to making beer

1 Crushed malt is mixed with hot water in a large tank called a mash tun.

2 The 'mash' sits at 65°C for 60 minutes to let the enzymes break down the starches from the malt into sugars.

3 The sweet liquid is separated from the crushed malt and pumped into a large tank for heating (a 'copper' or 'kettle').

4 The liquid is then boiled for another 60 minutes. Hops are added at precise times during the boil to add bitterness, aroma and flavour.

5 The boiled liquid (wort) is then cooled and pumped into a fermenting vessel.

6 Yeast is added to the mixture and briefly aerated.

7 Over the next 5–7 days, the yeast ferments the wort. The fermentation process is complete when all the sugars have been converted into alcohol and CO_2.

8 The new beer is cooled again to allow the yeast to settle.

9 The beer is pumped into conditioning tanks or casks for ageing.

10 After enough time has passed to mature the beer, and enough carbon dioxide has been added, the beer is ready for drinking.

How wine is made

When you buy a bottle of wine, you buy it because it tastes good. Okay, so the label might have had something to do with your choice, but a label can't win over your taste buds. The grape variety used is the main factor in determining the taste of a wine. And it's what happens to those grapes and their long journey from vine to glass that shapes its identity.

There's a whole lot of science going on behind where the grapes grow, and how they grow, but I'd need more space than I've got here to talk about that so I'm jumping forward to how wine is made. It actually doesn't take much. As soon as the skin on a grape splits open, the yeasts that live naturally in the air start doing their bit, converting the sugars to alcohol in a process called fermentation. This is where the winemakers come in. They control fermentation so the wine tastes the way they want it to.

If the winemaker is going for a lighter, unwooded style of dry white wine, the grapes are first crushed and separated from their stalks by a de-stemmer or crusher. Sulphur dioxide is added to prevent the juice oxidising and spoiling. Then the crushed grapes are pressed, leaving the skins behind. The resulting juice is pumped into a cold stainless-steel tank to settle. Yeast is added. Fermentation begins.

Red wine is made a little differently. If you were to press red grapes and leave the skins behind you would get white wine. The point is the skins. Ferment the juice together with the skins of red grapes and the colour and flavour emerge. Fermentation takes about four weeks or longer to complete. Once it's over, the new red wine is separated from its skins and pumped into barrels.

Fermentation of white wine, meanwhile, only takes a few days. The wine is then pumped off its lees (the spent yeast cells in the bottom of the tank) into another tank, where the temperature is brought down, a clarifying agent is added, and sugar is sometimes added too, if the weather hasn't been playing ball – or tartaric or citric acid might be added if there isn't enough acidity. The wine is then filtered and bottled.

If the winemaker is making a full-bodied, wooded dry white wine, then before fermentation is finished the wine is pumped into oak barrels, where it stays for six to eight months before being pumped back into tanks as before. Winemakers will do this for some red wines, too – to squeeze a bit more colour and flavour from the skins. It's called barrel fermentation.

Cue oak. It's the second most important ingredient in winemaking after the grape itself. Think of it as the magic ingredient – it can impart flavour, colour and tannin to a wine. Barrels cost a lot of dosh, and there is a pecking order of quality, with French oak barrels having the best reputation and the highest prices.

The level of toasting inside the barrels plays a part, too. It's a flavour enhancer. A light toast means the barrel is likely to add more oak flavour and tannins to a wine.

Heavily toasted barrels can add their own kind of caramelised flavours. The newer the barrel, the more oak flavour and tannin it gives to a wine.

Red wine spends more time in oak than white – usually nine to 18 months, depending on how much body and structure the winemaker is going for. But light quaffing reds for immediate consumption (most likely the wine you will be drinking on board) are invariably left in stainless-steel or concrete tanks.

If you like pink wines, you might like to know that they are made just like white wines, except that the juice is lightly tinted from a short contact with red skins before fermentation. Another way of making rosé is to bleed off the juice of a vat of crushed red grapes soon after fermentation has started.

Natural wines

An increasing number of winemakers are trying to do as little as possible to their wines. I'm talking natural wine – those made with little intervention, eschewing chemicals both in the vineyard and the winery and using the bare minimum of additives, or none at all. But it's the funky, feral aromas and oxidised palate of the more extreme natural wines that have prompted wide debate in the wine industry – its critics dismissing them as faulty and undrinkable, with the harshest words reserved for the whites (I'm a fan). The spectrum of natural wines ranges confusingly from cloudy, earthy and feral to vibrant, fruity and elegant, and many are just there for glugging, made with the sole purpose of expressing the most primary fruit possible. To the converts, it's the so-called faults that imbue the wine with its character. Where are they made? Pretty much all over the wine world these days. France tops the list, with natural wine hotspots from the Roussillon and the Loire to Alsace and Burgundy.

You want to know how fizz is made?

The classic – and best – way is called *méthode traditionelle*, which is used for Champagne, cava, Crémant and a few others, as it makes sparkling wine with more complex, toasty flavours. Blend your base wines (whole bunches gently pressed and fermented with yeast to make an unwooded dry white wine, which is then blended with other base wines, some made from the year or two before) with a little yeast and sugar. Then bottle it, cellar it, and wait for secondary fermentation – at least 18 months. The sediment is then shaken down and removed, the wine is topped up with more of the same wine, a little liquid sugar is added, it's corked, and left to settle for a few months before being sold.

You like your wines sweet?

We have rot to thank for the best stuff – or rather noble rot, aka *Botrytis cinerea*. It sets in when the grapes are picked late, drying them out and increasing their sugar content and acidity, adding glycerol (that luscious, syrupy texture) and a host of new flavours. It's back-breaking stuff as the grapes are picked by hand. They are crushed and pressed and yeast added, then the wine is put into stainless steel or oak and left for a few months, before being stabilised, fined and filtered, and bottled.

Enjoy a tipple of sherry, or port?

These fortified wines are the best-kept secret of the wine world. I'm a particular fan of sherry, which comes in two basic styles – pale, delicate fino and manzanilla (always in my fridge), and dark nutty amontillado and oloroso. The palomino grape rules in sherry land, in southern Spain. So does a natural yeast called flor, which gives sherry its unusual tang.

I love the way sherry is aged – in a unique *solera* system. Imagine a pyramid of barrels of different ages, with the oldest wine on the bottom layer and the youngest at the top. Every year, a bit of the wine from the bottom is taken away to be bottled and replaced by wine from the layer above, and so on. Do that in a hot, humid loft on the island of Madeira and you've got a wine called, er, Madeira. Now there's a wine for a boat if ever there was – it's indestructible.

Index

A

Absolut vodka 86
Andalucía, Spain 68
Adelaide Hills, Australia 96
Aegean Islands, Greece 75
agave nectar 15
alcohol units 21
Alentejo, Portugal 43
Amsterdam, Netherlands 31
Angostura bitters 15, 26
Aperol Spritz 65
Apple and Elderflower Spritz 161
apple brandy 34
Apple Mac 143
Aqua bar, Hong Kong 105
aquavit
    Denmark 82–3
    Sweden 87
Arran distillery, Scotland 40
artichoke, feta and ham tart 38
Asturias, Spain 40–1
Atlantic 22
    see also individual destinations
        by name
Australia 93, 94–7

B

bàcari, Venetian 64
Bairrada, Portugal 43
Baltic 81
    see also individual destinations
        by name
Bamford, Emma 117
bar spoons 12
Barbados 118–19, 127
Barossa, Australia 96
barrels, wine 169–70
bars in Hong Kong, best 105
Basque country wines 40
beer
    by country
        Australia 95
        Britain 27
        Denmark 82
        Holland 31
        Jersey 33
        Russia 91

Sweden 86
USA 48, 93, 111
how beer is made 167
bitters 15, 26
black bean salsa 50
black polenta, sundried tomato and
    mozzarella 66
Bloody Mary 151
books, boat drinker's 19
Bordeaux, France 37
Bornholm, Denmark 83
Boston cocktail shaker 13
bottle openers 12
brandy
    Calvados 34
    Cognac 36–7
    marc 57
breweries
    Australia 95
    Denmark 82
    East Coast, USA 48
    Germany 85
    Sweden 86
Bridgetown, Barbados 119
Britain 24–7, 30, 132
British Columbia, Canada 93, 102
British Royal Navy 26, 117, 127,
    133, 134
British Virgin Islands 116–17, 130

C

caffeine 21
Calabrese, Salvatore, 19, 153
California 93, 110–11
Callwood distillery, Tortola, BVI
    116–17
Campania, Italy 63
Canada 102
Canary Islands 46
Caribbean 112, 126
    see also individual destinations
        by name
Carlsberg brewery 82
Catalonia, Spain 69
cava 69, 170
celery salt 17
Central Coast, California 110
Chamonix Warwick Estate,
    South Africa 53
Champagne 24–5, 57, 170
Channel Islands 32–3

Château de Berne, Lorgues, France 57
chicken satay 108
chopping boards 12
Christian Drouin distillery,
    Normandy, France 34
cider
    Asturias, Spain 40–1
    Jersey and Guernsey 33
    Normandy, France 35
citrus squeezers 12
Clarke's Court distillery, Grenada 115
Cloudy Bay, Sauvignon Blanc 99
cloudy wine 20
cobbler cocktail shaker 13
cocktail shakers 13
cocktail sticks 13
cocktails 123–4
    Apple and Elderflower Spritz 161
    Apple Mac 143
    Bloody Mary 151
    Collins 135
    Cucumber Smash 165
    Dark & Stormy 131
    Death in the Afternoon 57
    gin 135–7, 139
    Gin Gin Mule 139
    Grenadian Kiss 115
    Gunner 104, 161
    Hoi Long 104
    John Collins 135
    Margarita 154, 156
    Mayan Mule 156
    Mojito 130
    Moscow Mule 150
    Mother's Milk 49
    Negroni 65, 136
    non-alcoholic 160–2, 165
    Painkiller 116, 130
    Paloma 157
    Piña Colada 131
    Pink Lady 136
    Rob Roy 65, 144
    rum 127, 128, 130–1
    Rum Punch 128
    Salty Dog 151
    Sangrita 162
    Saoco 49
    Sea Breeze 153
    Shirley Temple 162
    Silver Bullet 137
    Singapore Sling 106–7

Tequila Sunrise 157
Tom Collins 135
Veracruzana 158
vodka 150–1, 153
Vodka Gimlet 150
Walking Earl 146
whisky 143–6
Whisky Smash 145
Whisky Sour 144
coconut milk 17
coffee 87, 91
Cognac 36–7
Collins 135
Constantia, South Africa 53
Coonawarra, Australia 97
cordial, lime 17
corked wine 20
corks 19, 20
corkscrews 13
Corsica, France 60–1
Craddock, Harry 18, 19
craft beer
    East Coast, USA 48
    Holland 27
    Martinborough, New Zealand 99
    San Diego, California 93, 111
Crete, Greece 75
Croatia 72–3
Cuba 127, 130
Cucumber Smash 165
cures for hangovers 21, 151

D
Dansk Vincenter vineyard,
    Denmark 83
Dao, Portugal 43
Dark & Stormy 131
dehydration 21
Denmark 81, 82
dim sum 105
distilleries
    Barbados 119
    Britain 132, 133
    British Virgin Islands 116–17
    Channel Islands 33
    France 34
    Grenada 114–15
    Holland 31
    Ireland 142
    Isle of Wight 27
    Russia 91

Scotland 30, 140–1
Sweden 86
tequila 155
vodka 149
Douro, Portugal 43
drinking songs 86, 87

E
England 24–7
equipment, drink making 12–14

F
feta and olive bites 76
fika 87
Finger Lakes, USA 47
Florida Keys 48–9
Foursquare distillery, Barbados 119
France 34–7, 56–7, 60–1, 170
Franschhoek wine valley, South
    Africa 53
fruit juice 17

G
Galicia, Spain 41
garnishes, cocktail 124
genever (gin) 31, 133
Germany 81, 84–5
gin 132–3
    cocktails 135–7, 139
    eight facts about 134
    English 26, 132, 133
    genever 31, 133
    Guernsey 33
    how is gin made? 133
    Navy Strength 133
    Pink 26
    styles explained 134
Gin Gin Mule 139
ginger 17
ginger beer 95
glassware 13, 127
graters 12
gravadlax and beetroot 88
Great Southern, Australia 97
Greece 74–5
Green Parrot Bar, Whitehead
    Street, Florida Keys, USA 49
Grenada 114–15
grenadine 17
Guernsey 33
Gunner 104, 161

H
Hambledon vineyards, England 25
Hamburg, Germany 85
hangover cures 21, 151
Hemingway, Ernest 48, 49, 57, 130
HMS *Victory* 133
Holland 31–2
Honfleur harbour, Normandy,
    France 35
Hong Kong 93, 104–5
Hudson River, USA 47
Hunter Valley, Australia 97

I
ice 14
ice buckets 12
ice wines 102
Intercontinental Hotel, Hong Kong
    105
Irish Whiskey 142
Irouléguy, France 37
Isle of Wight 27
Istria, Croatia 72–3
Italy 62–5

J
jerked fish skewers and chutney
    mayo 120
Jersey 32
jiggers 12, 124
jugs 12

K
Key West, Florida Keys 48–9
kit, drink making 12–14
knives 14
Knox-Johnston, Sir Robin 140
kvas 81, 91

L
La Geria, Lanzarote 46
La Mare Wine Estate, Jersey 33
lager *see* beer
Languedoc, France 57
Lanzarote 46
lime cordial 17
Lobby Lounge, Intercontinental
    Hotel, Hong Kong 105
locker ingredients, boat 15, 17–18
Loire, France 35–6
London Dry gin 134

Long Bar, Raffles Hotel, Singapore 106–7
Long Island, New York State, USA 47
Los Olivos, Santa Barbara, USA 111
Loseby, Pat 104

M

Macedonia 75
Madeira 43, 171
Maison des Vins Côtes de Provence, Les Arcs sur Argens, France 57
Mallorca, Spain 69
Margaret River, Australia 96
Margaritas 154, 156
Marlborough, New Zealand 99
Martinborough, New Zealand 99
Maryland, USA 47
mauby 119
Mayan Mule 156
McLaren Vale, Australia 97
measuring cocktails 124
medications 21
Mediterranean 55
    see also individual destinations by name
Mexico 154, 155
mezcal 155
milk tea 105
Minho, Portugal 43
mixers 17
Mojito 130
Montenegro 73
Mornington Peninsula, Australia 97
mors 91
Moscow Mule 150
Mosel, Germany 85
Mother's Milk 49
Mount Etna, Sicily 63
muddlers 14, 124

N

Napa Valley, USA 111
Negroni 65, 136
New York State, USA 47
New Zealand 93, 99
non-alcoholic drinks
    batidos 49

cocktails 160–2, 165
coffee 87, 91
ginger beer 95
kvas 81, 91
mauby 119
milk tea 105
mors 91
Normandy, France 34
Nutbourne vineyards, England 25
nutmeg 17

O

Ocean bar, Hong Kong 105
Okanagan, Canada 102–3
oloroso 68
Ontario, Canada 102
ouzo 75
oxidation, wine 19, 20
Ozone bar at Ritz-Carlton, Hong Kong 105

P

Pacific 93
    see also individual destinations by name
Painkiller 116, 130
Palma, Mallorca, Spain 69
Paloma 157
pasta and vodka 149
pastis 57
Pays d'Auge, Normandy, France 34, 35
Penèdes, Spain 69
pepper mills 14
Piedmont, Italy 62, 65
Piña Colada 131
Pink Gin 26
Pink Lady 136
Poland 90, 148, 149
port 42–3, 171
Portixol, Palma Bay, Spain 69
Portugal 42–3
potted shrimps 28–9
preservation, wine 14
prohibition, USA 49, 127, 135, 142
Prosecco 64
Provence, France 56–7
Puglia, Italy 63
Pusser's Rum 112, 117

R

Raffles Hotel, Singapore 106–7
raki 79
Rathfinny Estate, England 25
rebujito 68
recipes for nibbles
    artichoke, feta and ham tart 38
    black bean salsa 50
    black polenta, sundried tomato and mozzarella 66
    cheat's chicken satay 108
    feta and olive bites 76
    gravadlax and beetroot 88
    jerked fish skewers and chutney mayo 120
    potted shrimps 27
    sardine-stuffed eggs 44
    stuffed mussels with parsley, garlic and Parmesan 100
    tuna-stuffed piquillo peppers 70
    two-olive tapenade 58
rehydration drinks 21
Republic of Singapore Yacht Club 107
Rheinessen, Germany 85
Rheingau, Germany 85
Rias Baixas, Galicia, Spain 41
Riebeek Kasteel, South Africa 53
River Antoine distillery, Grenada 114
Rob Roy 65, 144
root ginger 17
Rotterdam, Netherlands 31
Roussillon, France 57
Royal Hong Kong Yacht Club 104
Royal Navy rum 117
rum 112, 126–7
    Australia 95
    Barbados 118–19
    British Virgin Islands 116–17
    cocktails 128, 130–1
    eight facts about 127
    Florida Keys 49
    Grenada 114–15
    how is rum made? 126–7
Rum Runners 49
Russia 81, 90–1, 148, 149

S

salt 17
Salty Dog 151
Sámos, Greece 75

San Diego, USA 93, 111
San Francisco, USA 111
Sangrita 162
Santa Barbara, USA 110–11
Santa Maria Valley, USA 110
Santa Ynez Valley, USA 110–11
Santorini, Greece 75
Saoco 49
sardine-stuffed eggs 44
Sardinia, Italy 63
Sark 33
Sauvignon Blanc 99
Schuhmachers beer garden,
    Hamburg 85
Scotch *see* whisky
Scotland 30
screw cap wine bottles 19, 20
Sea Breeze 153
Sevva bar, Hong Kong 105
sherry 68, 171
Shirley Temple 162
Shoalhaven Coast, Australia 96
Sicily 63
Silver Bullet 137
Singapore 93, 106–7
Singapore Sling 106–7
Sloppy Joe's bar, Whitehead
    Street, Florida Keys, USA 49
Smith, Lars Olsson 86
snaps 82, 87
songs, Swedish drinking 86, 87
Sonoma, USA 111
South Africa 53
Spain 40–1, 68–9, 134, 171
sparkling wine
    cava 69
    England 24–5
    how is fizz made? 170
    Prosecco 64
spirit measures 12, 124
St Nicholas Abbey distillery,
    Barbados 119
Stock Island, Florida Keys, USA 49
strainers, cocktail 13, 14
straws 14
stuffed mussels with parsley, garlic
    and Parmesan 100
sugar cane 112, 126, 127
sugar syrup 17–18
Swartland, South Africa 53
Sweden 81, 86, 149

T
tabasco 18
tartrates 20
Tasmania, Australia 97
tea 105, 146
tequila 154
    cocktails 156–8
    how is tequila made? 155
    what is tequila 155
Tequila Sunrise 157
Tim Ho Wan, Kowloon 105
Tobermory distillery, Scotland 30
tongs 14
tonics 17
Tortola, British Virgin Islands 112,
    116–17
tuna-stuffed piquillo peppers 70
Turkey 78–9
Tuscany, Italy 63
twists, cocktail 124
two-olive tapenade 58
Txakoli 40

U
United States of America
    East Coast 47–8
    Florida Keys 48–9
    prohibition 49, 127, 135, 142
    West Coast 110–11
units, alcohol 21

V
Valdeorras, Spain 41
Venetian bàcari, Italy 64
Veneto, Italy 64
Veracruzana 158
Verdicchio, Italy 64
vermouth 65
Vila Nova de Gaia, Portugal
    43
Vineyards *see* wines
virgin cocktails 160–2, 165
Virgin Islands, British 116–17
Virginia, USA 47–8
vodka
    cocktails 150–1, 153
    eight facts about 149
    how is vodka made? 148–9
    Poland 90, 148, 149
    Russia 81, 90–1, 148, 149
    Sweden 86, 149

Vodka Gimlet 150
Vouvray, Loire, France 36

W
Walking Earl 146
whisky 30
    cocktails 143–6
    history 140–1
    how is malt whisky made? 142
    Irish Whiskey 142
    Whisky Smash 145
    Whisky Sour 144
wine
    corks and screw caps 19–20
    by country
        Australia 93, 94–7
        Canada 102
        Canary Islands 46
        Corsica 60–1
        Croatia 72–3
        Denmark 81, 83
        England 24–5
        France 35–7, 56–7, 60–1
        Germany 81, 84–5
        Greece 74–5
        Italy 62–4
        Jersey 32, 33
        Montenegro 73
        New Zealand 93, 99
        Portugal 43
        South Africa 53
        Spain 40, 41, 69
        Sweden 81
        Turkey 78
        United States of America
            47–8, 93, 110–11
    faults and how to spot them 20
    how is wine made? 168–71
    ice 102
    natural 170
    preservation 14
    sparkling 24–5, 64, 69, 170
Worcestershire sauce 18

Y
yum cha 105

Z
zocos 46

Acknowledgements

This book would not have been possible without a little coaxing from Clara Jump and Jenny Clark, and the rest of the team at Bloomsbury/Adlard Coles – always a pleasure doing business with you, ladies.

And big thanks again to my mentor and dear mate Fiona Beckett for being a sounding board, for giving me a shove when needed, and for reining me in when I get carried away. Thanks go, too, to my gorgeous husband, who supported me throughout, even though he gets queasy at the mere thought of being on the water.

And blessings, once again, to the UK's most famous sailor, Sir Robin Knox-Johnston, who shared with me his Headland Policy (it involves whisky) and to another illustrious sailor, Emma Bamford, for contributing a drinking story par excellence (involving copious cocktails in the BVI).

I gratefully acknowledge, too, all those top bartenders, chefs, food writers, brewers, distillers and winemakers who continue to inspire me, as I travel around the world.

It was ace photographer Julian Winslow who brought those boat nibble recipes to life on the page, while Louise Sheeran added another layer of creativity with the best boat drinks book illustrations ever.

And those boat nibble recipes wouldn't have looked quite so sexy without the help of brilliant chef Jay Amado Santiago, who cooks at my favourite Isle of Wight eatery, The Little Gloster.

Nor would the photo shoot have gone quite so smoothly without the energy of dear mates Ria King and Alison Whitewood, whose Yarmouth boutique Blue continues to be a source of inspiration, not to mention props for this book. And I must tip my hat to Yarmouth Harbour Master Tim Adams, who let us run riot around the marina snapping pics.

Finally, and most importantly, thanks to my wonderful parents for giving me a love of the sea, and to dad for your offer-of-the-week wines, which motivated me to write this book.

Picture credits All photographs are © Julian Winslow with the exception of the following:

p31 © Gabriel Perez, Getty Images, p32 © Michael Runkel, Getty Images, p34 © Joas Souza Photographer - joasphotographer.com, Getty Images; p37 © Tim Graham, Getty Images; pp40–1 © Santiago Urquijo, Getty Images; p42 © Michele Falzone, Getty Images; p47 © Dennis Macdonald, Getty Images, pp48–9 © Randy Wells, Getty Images; p52 © Marc Hoberman, Getty Images; p56 © Brian Jannsen, Getty Images; p60–1 © Benslimanhassen, iStock; p62 © Andrea Pistolesi, Getty Images; p65 © Giorgio Fochesato, Getty Images; p74 © Danita Delimont, Getty Images; p78 © Ugurhan Betin, iStock; p87 © Martin Wahlborg, iStock; p91 © Mr Anujak Jaimook, Getty Images; p95 © Cretex, Getty Images; pp96–7 © Andrey Moisseyev, iStock; p98 © iShootPhotosLLC, iStock; p103 © Claude Robidoux, Getty Images; p104 © Tom Bonaventure, Getty Images; p105 © Matteo Colombo, Getty Images; p107 © Amanda Hall, Getty Images; pp110–1 © Panoramic Images, Getty Images; pp114–5 © Argalis, Getty Images; p117 © Reed Kaestner, Getty Images; pp118–9 © Westend61, Getty Images; p119 © Jonathan Blair, Getty Images; p126 © altrendo images, Getty Images; p134 © LianeM, iStock; pp140–1 © ra-photos, iStock; p142 © drserg, iStock; p154 © Mark D Callanan, Getty Images; p168 © Jim Kruger, Getty Images; p169 © Michel de Leeuw, Getty Images; pp170–1 © Tostphoto, iStock

Background and effects © Shutterstock, iStock and Getty Images

Coal House Diary

You know who you are, and what you have done for me. Thank you.

an imprint of Gomer Press,
Llandysul, Ceredigion SA44 4JL
www.gomer.co.uk

ISBN 978 1 84323 994 9

A CIP record for this title is available from the British Library

Design: mopublications.com

This book is published with the financial support of the Welsh Books Council.

Printed and bound in Wales at Gomer Press, Llandysul, Ceredigion SA44 4JL

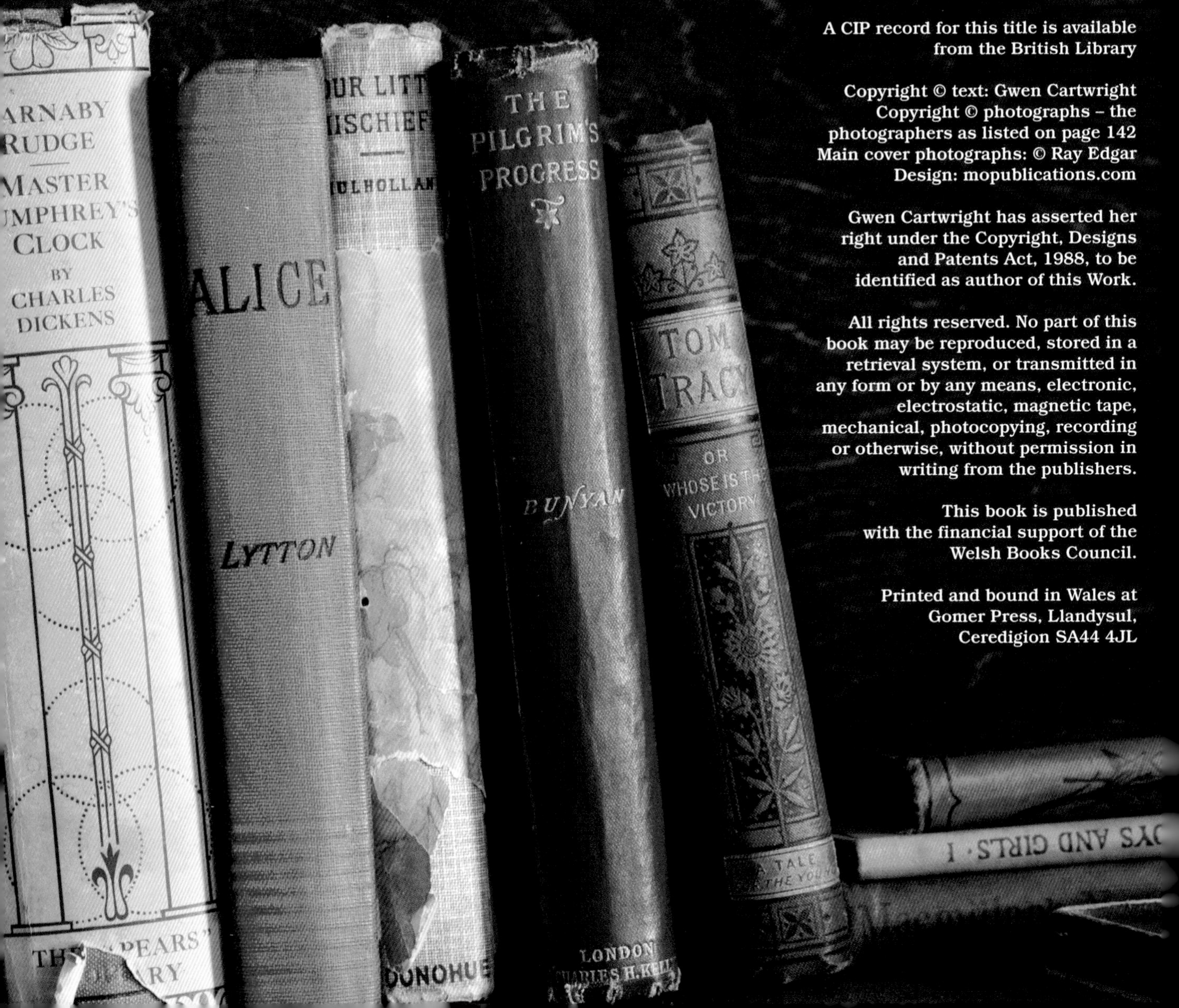

Gwen Cartwright

Coal House Diary

Pont

Contents

Gwen's Diary   9

All in a Day's Work   40

Back to School   56

Men and Bosses   72

All Work and No Play   106

Goodbye   136

Who's Who?   140

Acknowledgements   142

Arriving in 1927 ... the Phillipses, the Cartwrights and the Griffithses

Dear Diary,
Today I travelled back
in time! To 1927!

I think I need to explain: I'm taking part in a project for BBC Wales called *Coal House*. For a whole month three families: the Cartwrights (us), the Griffithses and the Phillipses are going to live as if it is really 1927. We'll have to dress in authentic 1927 clothes, and the dads – and some of the older boys – will work in a coal mine. The mums will stay at home in Stack Square and look after the house and the children. We'll only be able to buy stuff which was on sale at the time – and we'll be using old money: pounds, shillings and pence. We're going to have to live without all kinds of modern conveniences.

All plaited up

I don't know what we'll do without TV! We won't even have a bathroom! Worse luck, the children will still have to go to school but at least the lessons will be a bit different.

This morning we all had to get up at 6.30 to travel (in a car, in modern clothes) to the old cottages at Stack Square in Blaenafon which is close to Big Pit Mining Museum.

Once we arrived, Mum, Dad, Kitty and I were given a parcel with our clothing for the next four weeks. I had to wear a petticoat, dress, apron, woolly hat, socks and shoes. The underwear's really gross – baggy knickers – and the cardigans are so itchy that I'm not going to wear mine. After dressing, I took off my nail polish and make-up and my hair was plaited with elastic bands and tied with burgundy ribbon. After four weeks, I guess it will be all greasy with split ends! Dad's had to have a different hairstyle too, and he's even grown a moustache.

The tai bach

After getting into costume, we went into our cottage, which is tiny. There are only four rooms in the whole house: a kitchen/dining/living room, a social room with a piano and a chest of drawers to put our clothes in, plus two bedrooms, one with a double bed for my parents, and another room for Kitty and me. Just two single beds, a chair, and a wash-stand by the window!

In the kitchen there's a range (we'll have to cook with this) and on the table were some provisions to start off with; we will have to buy our food in the future. We have to share outside-toilets with the other families, the Phillipses and the Griffithses.

After looking round the cottages with the others, I decided I needed the loo, so Jade (from Number 8), Angharad (from Number 6) and I went round the back of the houses to try them out. I don't want to go into graphic detail but it goes without saying that they were not nice! You do

Lights out

your business into a hole but there is no flush so it just stays there. Then, as they didn't have loo-roll in 1927, you have to use old newspaper instead. Yuk!

We went back to our 'new' homes, wondering what else was in store for us. For tea, which took an hour and a half to cook, we had fried potatoes with onions and carrots. It only scored four out of ten! Mum originally planned to make corned beef hash but using the corned beef would have added another hour onto the cooking time because the range, Mr O'Brien as Mum calls it, makes everything take a lot longer than on a modern cooker.

Last thing before going to bed (much earlier than at home and so much darker without electric light), I took off my many layers of clothes to change into my nightie. I got into bed to write my diary absolutely exhausted . . . and it is only the first day!

Gwen

16 October 1927

Waking up in a different place was strange

but at least I had an extra ten minutes in bed this morning. I got up at 6.40 instead of 6.30! It was weird seeing Mum, Dad and Kitty in their old-fashioned clothes. For breakfast we used some leftover potatoes and onions from last night's dinner to make an omelette.

Afterwards, I realised I really needed the loo but I didn't have my shoes on (they take ages to do up) so I had to use the chamber pot in my room. Then I had to empty it out in the *tŷ bach*. What a yucky job! One for Mum, I think, in future. Poor her!

Pepper and Salt
the Coal House pigs

Kitty and I fed the pigs and chickens (a good idea) and then all of us children decided to let the pigs out into the yard (not such a good idea)! They went crazy! Back home, my dog Bertie sometimes goes hyper and starts running as fast as he can around the living-room table. We call it 'going crackerdog'. Well, the pigs were definitely 'going crackerpig'! We managed to tempt Salt (one of them) back into the sty with food but this made Pepper (the other one) go mad, so the adults had to put him in the sty for us. There are six adults altogether and a total of eleven children.

For lunch, we had bread and butter with jam and apricot chutney. At 1.30 Dad and the other men went off to the mine for the very first time. It's an hour and a half each way – four miles and lots of hills – I don't envy them. About half an hour after they left, it started raining. Poor Dad. Me and Mum made a meat stew with carrots and swede and we put it on to cook, hoping it would last us a few meals.

Oh, Rhodri!

I did about three hours of jobs: cooking, poking the fire and sweeping, while Kitty stayed next door, chatting to Jade and Angharad. Unfair! We all need to do the same amount of jobs, I think.

In a break from work, I made some orange squash, using orange zest, juice, sugar and water. I drained it through the tea strainer and tried a bit and it was quite nice but very sweet. The water out of the pump tastes really weird and Angharad refuses to drink it, so I decided I would give her my orange juice. As I was coming back from next door, two-year-old Rhodri Phillips decided to stick his foot in the drip bucket under the water pump so I picked him up and took him to his mum. She was quite upset because Rhodri got his shoes wet and he only has one pair.

I went back inside our cottage and as soon as I entered the kitchen I heard a cry of 'GROCER!' Mike (that's the

grocer's name) is going to call at Stack Square regularly so that we can buy things from him. Mum bought some dried mixed fruit and some bread. Altogether it cost sixpence in old-fashioned money but we only had five pennies so we had to 'borrow' one penny from the rent money. As we don't know when the rent man will call, we felt a bit nervous because he could come at any time and we won't be able to pay him.

Mum made some Bara Brith with our fruit but the oven wasn't hot enough to cook it. We had to put it in a stew pot on top of the range to get it started. Mum says that Bara Brith and a sandwich is going to be Dad's lunch every day! Because she needed to start boiling the potatoes on top of the range, I put the mixture back in the oven. If it didn't cook, we were going to drop blobs of dough onto the bakestone and make Bara Brith Welsh cakes! I put it in at two o'clock and by four o'clock it still hadn't done anything, but when Mum

'Old' money

opened the oven at eight (to resort to the Welsh-cake plan), it had just started cooking.

Dad came home absolutely chilled to the bone as he had been working above ground in the rain. He was half an hour too early for us so his tea wasn't ready and the water wasn't hot, which made him grouchy. But it wasn't our fault! Everything takes so long! Half an hour after he got home, we ate our stew, with potatoes fried in lard. It was all right. We ate all of the stew, which was supposed to last three meals. I think we were really hungry because of all the work we've done today. Mum has put some dried peas on the sideboard to soak for a pea soup.

We're going to school for the first time tomorrow but none of us knows who our teacher is yet. About nine o'clock we heard a knock next door. We tried to work out what was going on but all we could hear was muffled talking and the steady patter of the rain.

An oil lamp –
one of many

Angharad Griffiths came round about half an hour later to tell us that they have got a lodger called Mr Michaels. Apparently he's the headmaster of our school. His arrival has got Debra Griffiths, Angharad's mum, all flustered, which made her drop a lamp. The one we lent her! Whoops! We have still got about one million lamps though.

Gwen

P.S. THE BARA BRITH WORKED, HURRAH! It was all my mum's work though it was Debra's recipe.

17 October 1927

I got up at 6.30 a.m. again today

Dad made me and Kitty try some porridge for breakfast. I had a bit and thought it was too bland so I put in some currants, lashings of golden syrup and a mound of sugar – and my dad said porridge was healthy! I ate about half of it and decided I was full but Dad said I had to eat it all! I did, even though I was forcing it down at the end, but Kitty got told off because she wouldn't eat hers. Dad doesn't seem to think that we are allowed not to like something.

Mum started making pea soup for our lunch but I think it's going to taste a bit weird as she's using dried peas.

Dad went off to work at the mine. I put on my navy coat and then all the children, except Jade and Ryan (too old),

Our school

and Rhodri and Gwennan (too young), set off for school. It only took five minutes to walk there. We played a wall game in the yard, girls versus boys, which involved trying to kick the football from one side of the yard to the other.

Our teacher came out to take us inside the school for our first lessons. It was Mr Michaels, the teacher staying with the Griffithses; we had thought he was our headmaster. We lined up against the wall and I gave him my friendliest grin, but he just told me to stop smiling. Oh!

He went through all the school rules . . . and then the punishments for disobeying them. We might get detention (where we would have to write lines), he might send a letter home to our parents or, worst of all, we might get the Cane!

Lessons are going to be so different! This morning we learnt about the British Empire and saw all the

countries ruled by Britain coloured pink on an old map. Then we learnt about how the Great War started. We cannot call it the First World War because back in 1927 there hadn't been a second one! Then we learnt our two- and three-times tables even though I already knew them. Then we went home for lunch – two whole hours.

We had bread and butter followed by drop scones with treacle instead of the pea soup, because Mum is going to use it for dinner tonight with some faggots she bought from the butcher. He called while we were at school. As well as the faggots, Mum got some stewing beef and brawn. She made us laugh by telling us that Debra's fire kept going out and that, while she was poking it, the grate fell to pieces. Mum and Debra managed to fix it but were left with an extra bit of grate which they couldn't fit anywhere.

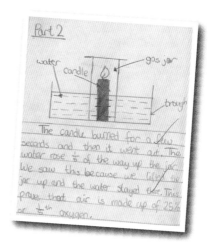

In the afternoon at school we did science and learnt about combustion. 'Combustion' means 'burning' and we did some really flashy experiments with a candle, water and a jar.

We came home a quarter of an hour early and worked flat out for an hour in the house. Then Dad got home early too, demanding a cup of tea and not realising it would take us half an hour to boil the kettle . . . which would make dinner even later. Me and Kitty were really hungry but we didn't complain because Dad looked exhausted. An hour late we had our faggots, pea soup and mashed potatoes.

Later we went next door to the Phillipses to hear a radio broadcast about the possibility of putting in pithead baths at the mine. I think it's a good idea because it would save us having to get lots of water ready for when Dad gets home. We came back from Number 8

Chickens!

Stack Square and had some stewed apples with drop scones. Me and Kitty had an argument because I said she wasn't doing any jobs, just sitting around in Number 6 and Number 8. Mum and Dad agreed with me, so tomorrow I get a bit of a day off while she does all the jobs I've been doing for the past few days.

The other children came into our house in the evening. We've made up a song on our piano which we're going to play for Debra on her fortieth birthday. When Kitty was playing the piano, she found a hymn which Angharad and I both know, so we're going to sing that for Debra's birthday too. Then we all went outside and played snakes and ladders in the dark.

Rhodri Phillips managed to get hold of a chicken and threw it in the air to 'see if it could fly'. Our family is doing the chickens this week which involves feeding them, giving them water and cleaning out their coop.

18 October 1927

I got up at 7.00 today, only to go downstairs and find Dad bleeding

and about to depart for hospital. I was glad that he was going to a modern A & E department, not the 1920s version! When he'd gone, Mum told me what happened. Apparently he had been shaving wood with a knife to try and get the fire started when he slipped and cut his hand.

We tried to get on as normal. I ate some bread with honey then went to school with the others (minus Steffan and Gethin because they are ill). We swapped teams for the wall game and I kicked the football over the wall twice. It's annoying when it rolls down the hill.

Over the wall

Lesson time

In the morning we did some history and coloured some maps showing Germany and Austria before and after the War. Then we chose either water or milk before going out to play. After break we did English and learnt about phrases and sentences.

We came home for lunch and I had more bread and honey; it's becoming quite a habit. Debra's fire is working again but it won't be for long! Gethin and Steffan are still really ill and couldn't come to school this afternoon either.

We did maths all afternoon. We were learning how to use old-fashioned money: £ s d, which is very confusing. I can see why we switched to pounds and pence.

When we got home, Dad was back from hospital. He was fine and he was painting pictures, sitting on the wall. Mum said he was out there because otherwise he

was in the way of the women, who were trying to get on with things. Dad thinks if he paints some good pictures he could swap them for some food.

All of us children let the pigs out and Jade cleaned their sty as that is one of the duties of the Pig Monitor. Salt and Pepper went crackerpig again but we let them be and they went back in the pig pen of their own accord (well we did have to use a bit of food as bait). Earlier on, Stephie (Jade's mum) had made a wooden sword for Rhodri but, while prodding the pigs with it, he dropped it in the pig pen . . . and they ate it. They will eat ANYTHING!

For dinner we had beef stew and and cabbagey mashed potato; there is still half the stew left. I made Debra's fortieth birthday card but it's not finished completely; it is going to be from all of us Cartwrights.

19 October 1927

Got up at 7.10 today and had more porridge and golden syrup for breakfast

When we got to school we did some poetry in Welsh. We're going to perform it as a class in the Hunger March concert. (They held Hunger Marches in 1927 to protest about the government not giving help to unemployed miners.) Then we all did painting – flowers – and I did another card for Debra and then we all came home for lunch. Me and Mum had brawn sandwiches but Kitty didn't want them because brawn is made from a pig's head. Mum had made the brawn into sausages and I had mine in a sandwich with lots of butter. They were really hot and yummy.

Joe underground

I like coming home for lunch because it breaks up the day. I like having a bit of rest and playtime in between school hours.

In the afternoon we carried on learning our poetry and I can do the first verse without the words. Then we learnt a bit about mining. We knelt under a bench at the back of the classroom and banged on the wall behind it with pretend mandrels and shovelled coal into pretend trams above our heads to get an idea of what our dads are doing when they are underground. It is very, very tiring.

We came home an hour and a half early because our teacher needed to catch the steam train to London. When we got home we made some Tinker's cakes – like apple Welsh cakes with no currants. They're so delicious, I nearly ate them all. Then we let the pigs out.

Joe at the surface

Mum started reheating the stew we had last night. We will have to eat all of it tonight because we cannot reheat it again. Things go off if you haven't got a fridge!

We got the tea ready for half past five but Dad didn't get home until 6.20. It's the first time he's been late home when we've been ready with the dinner, hot water and a cup of tea! The other families had fish and chips, lucky things, but Dad didn't get us any because they were too expensive. Dad's on half pay – because of his bad finger – and couldn't afford to spend 2s 6d (two shillings and sixpence) on fish and chips for us. The half pay and not being allowed down the mine with the other men is making Dad really grumpy.

We settled down to eat our stew when Richie Phillips (Rhodri's dad) knocked on our door and gave us a portion of fish and chips and then Cerdin Griffiths (Angharad's dad) did the same. Me and Kitty were very

A piggy rod in action

happy because it is one of the few treats we've had so far.

After dinner the children went outside; Ryan and Steffan were playing rugby and the little ones were playing with the pigs, which were still out. Kitty and Angharad started to make up a Morris Dance using two sticks each that our dads brought back from the mine. I tied some lengths of ribbon together to make a long multi-coloured piece and I'm making up a dance using it for Debra's birthday. The pigs tried to eat my ribbons and my shoelace.

Then the kids all made piggy rods which involve putting a bit of pig food on a length of string tied to a stick. Using these, you can make the pigs do tricks like spinning around and running really fast.

20 October 1927

Today we got up at 8.00 because our teacher's gone to a conference

Great – a lie in! The men only went to work for half a day which meant more time to get ready for the great event tonight, Debra's birthday. Steph has made her a pillow with a straw handle and Jade has embroidered a picture of the Blaenafon ironworks. We have made some more Tinker's cakes, a big one saying 40 on it in raisins and two small ones saying 4 and 0. I think Steph is going to make some more Welsh cakes and Richie has made some beer. We were going to make some sweets but the grocer's visit put paid to that idea as you will see.

Happy birthday

Many happy returns

First thing, Debra found that she was missing some bloomers and eventually we realised that the pigs must have eaten them. Mum was in hysterics. I made a model of a pig out of pipe cleaners and a model of a pair of bloomers on the line.

The grocer called at about ten with some really cheap sweets – and Debra bought some off him! As well as making coconut ice as a present, Mum had been thinking about making sweets to sell, but she couldn't compete with the grocer's prices. She is really downcast. Everybody got a bargain of some kind today – we had a discount of 1s 2d ('one and tuppence') altogether – but that was because it was the apprentice and not the grocer and I don't think he's too good with money. Debra got thruppence off some chocolate – as a birthday treat – and bought bags of sweets for the children! We're too poor to have a bag each like the others so me and Kitty had to share.

Smilers!

In the afternoon someone let the pigs out again – they are really scaring the chickens; this is probably why they aren't laying eggs. Later we got a charity food delivery: a huge vat of cawl. We're going to split it tomorrow and have it for dinner.

In the evening we had a party for Debra and a singsong round the piano which made little Gwennan Phillips do her big smile. Ah! We sang 'Seek Ye First the Kingdom of God'. First in Welsh, then in English. It made Debra cry. We made up our very own Coal House song, which included lines like 'The pigs ate Debra's bloomers; Rhodri doesn't like the pigs'. The Tinker's cakes and Welsh cakes were big successes and everyone ate loads. Debra loved all her cards and presents and the paintings we did in school. She said it was her best birthday ever. I wish I could have had my birthday in the Coal House!

All in a Day's Work

If working underground was back-breaking, work at home was often just as hard. Shortage of money meant that mothers would often go without food themselves to make sure there was enough for their husbands and children and, without modern appliances, the list of household tasks was endless. Gwen's mum did well to keep her family fed.

Keeping a good fire going was all-important. It not only warmed the house (in hot weather as well as cold), it also served to cook the food, and provided all the water for washing and bathing. Every drop of water had to be fetched from the pump in the Square.

Washing clothes and getting them dry and aired was a major operation. Filling the water tub with hot water and scrubbing clothes on the washboard was hard physical work, to say nothing of squeezing out the excess water in the mangle before pegging the clothes on the line, and bringing them back inside for ironing. No wonder Mum was so upset when Gwen fell over in a clean set of clothes.

Keeping the house clean and tidy was a big challenge when coal dust invaded every nook and cranny. Without a hoover, mats needed to be beaten and floors swept regularly. With not much money to spare, and a make-do-and-mend approach, at least the family couldn't clutter their home with an excess of consumer goods!

Electricity today means light at the flick of a switch, but in 1927 many houses still used oil lamps and candles. Dim light meant that it was harder to do chores in the winter evenings. Mum still kept busy though; a pile of mending awaited her when everyone else had finished their work – and, if she had nothing else to do, then she could always get on with her knitting. Annabel and Gwen both knitted during their time at Stack Square.

21 October 1927

We got up a bit late today

and just had some bread for breakfast and a pot of tea.

We found out that we had a half-day holiday from school – great! During the morning the butcher called and gave us sausages worth 1s 6d for just sixpence. Mum could only afford enough for Dad – who needs the protein – but the butcher gave her sausages for all of us.

Mum and Debra were discussing what to have with the sausages when they got onto the subject of eggs. It turns out that Dan Phillips found two yesterday but nobody got given any. We worked out that the pigs must have eaten them. After having a major egg hunt (when Rhodri found three in the feed shed), we finally let the pigs out.

Round the piano

The men came home at half past twelve for lunch (they were going rugby training this afternoon) and Richie made Rhodri a wooden gun. Trouble ahead!

We headed off to school with the football and had a singing lesson from Mr Whitcombe, the choir master. He's going to be teaching our dads too. Before we learnt some songs, we warmed up using Tonic Sol-fa (which involves using hand movements to go with the notes). I have been doing music since I was four but this was the first time I had come across Tonic Sol-fa. It's really interesting even though it took a while to learn the hand signals!

We also learnt the first verse of 'Ar Hyd y Nos'.

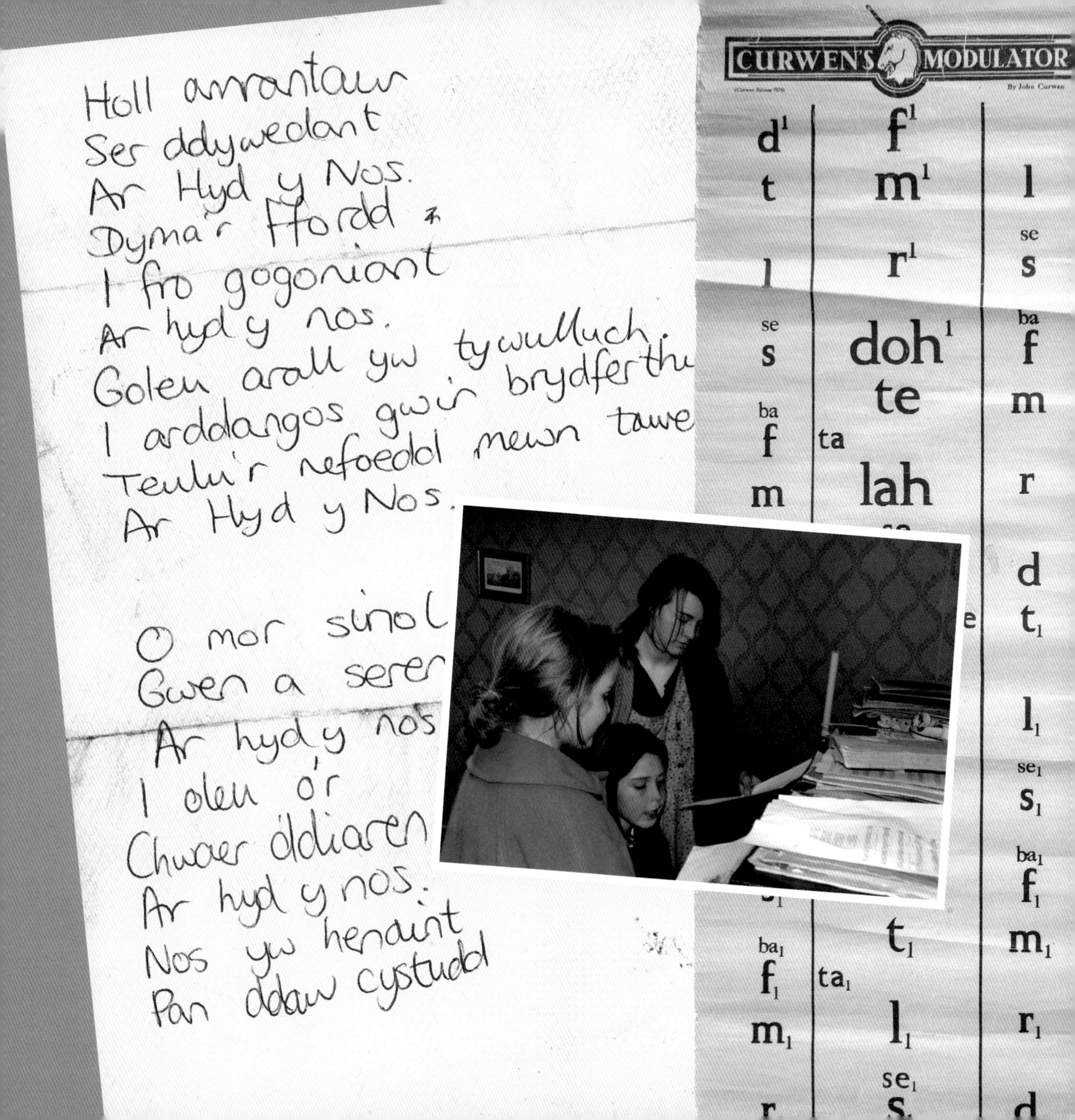

Holl amrantau
Ser ddywedant
Ar Hyd y Nos.
Dyma'r Ffordd
I fro gogoniant
Ar hyd y nos.
Goleu arall yw tywulluch
I arddangos gwir brydferthu
Teulu'r nefoedol mewn tawe
Ar Hyd y Nos.

O mor sirol
Gwen a serer
Ar hyd y nos
I olen o'r
Chwaer ddiaren
Ar hyd y nos.
Nos yw henaint
Pan ddaw cystudd

d¹	f¹ m¹	l
t	r¹	se
l		s
se	doh¹	ba
s	te	f
ba	ta	m
f	lah	r
m		d
		t₁
		l₁
	e	se₁
		s₁
		ba
		f₁
b₁		m₁
ba₁	t₁	
f₁	ta₁	
m₁	l₁	r₁
	se₁	d
	s₁	

Bara Brith

We also learnt the hymns 'Blessed Assurance' and 'What a Friend we have in Jesus'. After break Mr Michaels carried on teaching us pounds, shillings and pence in maths. I'm not too bad any more, only if there are very large numbers.

When we got home from school, Mum was busy making Bara Brith. We had cawl (donated by the church) for dinner with some bread and butter. Then we invited Daniel, Katie, Ryan and Angharad round to play cards.

Angharad told us what was wrong with Gethin and Steffan! Steffan is getting better from a bout of sickness but Gethin's got chickenpox. We went outside and had such a laugh in the yard, playing around with sticks, stones, a rugby ball and our football. Richie came out and joined us. He nearly broke a window, then hurried back inside and put the blame on Ryan! Dads!

Coal House
Cluedo cards

Back at Number 7, we helped get the Bara Brith out of the oven. Yum. We had some choc buttons out of our small sweetie stack in the butter dish. Double yum.

We've been making up games, including Coal House Cluedo. All six adults are suspects – we made them out of washing pegs cut in half and coloured with wax crayons. A can of paraffin, a washing line, undercooked faggots, a mandrel, an axe and a candlestick are the weapons. We drew these onto paper. Instead of the real Cluedo rooms, we decided on nine different locations: the toilets; coalshed; each of the houses; the pig and chicken pens and the feed shed. There is going to be a secret passage from our house to the toilets and another one from the feed shed to the pigs. All we need is a game board now.

We also made up a game called 'hunt the eggs' (which is very cool) and Rhodri really loves it.

22 October 1927

Dad was mad at Kitty this morning

because she wouldn't eat her porridge. He ranted at her: 'You'll have porridge or you won't have anything!' She hates it so much that she decided not to have anything. I ate all my porridge though I don't really like it.

When we went to school, there was still no Gethin because of his chickenpox. We did English and learnt about words which sound the same but mean different things. Like 'boy' and 'buoy'. Kitty used 'quay' as in Mermaid Quay (which wasn't around in 1927). At break, Sir cut us a long skipping rope which was really good fun. We played all sorts of games and tried

running in and out while two people turned the rope. I could run in but always tripped over on the way out.

After break we did maths: our six- and seven-times tables – easy peasy – and yet more money. Today it was subtraction – with halfpennies and farthings!

We had cheesy toast for lunch and then Debra came around asking for sugar. The second day in a row! Mum said yes but she'd have to give it back. The grocer had come whilst we were in school. Mum had bought wool (for two shillings) and knitting needles and a bag each of eating apples and cooking apples so after our cheesy toast we had stewed apples. Before going back to school, I started knitting a dishcloth. It's fifty-six stitches long.

In the afternoon we did two lots of history. We learnt about the death toll in the First World War. It really makes you think how much men were willing to risk for

their country. The losses at the Battle of the Somme were awesome – and I mean that in a bad way.

We also learnt some history about mining and how cheap German coal is going to threaten our dads' jobs. We drew a cross-section of a shaft mine. Mr Michaels had only just managed to persuade Steffan (13) and Daniel (8) that they should stay at school instead of going underground when a note arrived saying that Steffan would have to start work down the pit. Mr Michaels seemed really upset.

We had bacon stir fry for dinner with some cheese on top, and bread. Dad showed us the board he's found us for Cluedo. Kitty and I are going to colour it in and we're going to try to find a dice.

23 October 1927

I had a spoonful of golden syrup today

as a reward for eating all my porridge.

In school this morning we started preparing for our English homework. We have to write an essay about Lord Nelson so we wrote down lots of notes about him like when he was born, etc . . . It was quite good really.

At lunchtime – omelette with potatoes (four eggs found yesterday!) – I did some more knitting, before going back to school for maths. We were learning about imperial (old) length, which is really hard. Nothing so simple as centimetres in 1927!

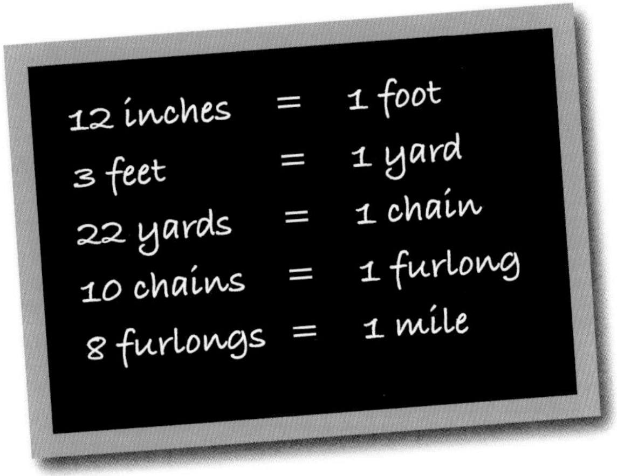

12 inches = 1 foot
3 feet = 1 yard
22 yards = 1 chain
10 chains = 1 furlong
8 furlongs = 1 mile

Old measures
of length

Then me and Kitty did some problems like working out how many inches there are in 1ft 5ins. The answer is 17 inches. (An inch, by the way, is the same as two-and-a-half centimetres.) After the maths we did some more mining history.

We got home to find out that we could go to the cinema if Dad had earned enough money to pay for our tickets. Luckily when he got home, he did have enough! Me and Mum made loads of Welsh cakes because Kitty put double the lard in the mixture so we had to double everything! We ate nearly all of them before Mum reminded us that Mr Michaels our teacher was coming round for dinner.

We invited him because the butcher had given us extra sausages so that we could afford to feed more mouths. We had sausage-and-onion gravy with mash, and swede-and-carrot puree, which was delicious. Then we

'Can we go, Dad?'

had some of the few leftover Welsh cakes with stewed apples.

We went to the cinema and me and Kitty got to have a bag of sweets <u>each</u> for one old penny per bag (that's less than half of one new penny). We watched the *Phantom of the Opera*. It was good but after a bit, the film started to freeze and went back to the beginning. It was a shame because I was starting to get into it. It was a silent film – just pictures – although there was a man playing the piano to add to the atmosphere. It was really good – but weird compared to 2007! Rhodri and Gwennan fell asleep in the cinema.

And now that we're back home, it won't be long before I'm fast asleep too.

Old Money — A Guide

d = old penny (pre decimalisation)

There were 20 shillings per pound (£1)

The shilling was subdivided into 12 pennies.

The penny was further subdivided into 2 half pennies.

therefore £1 = 24...

Award
for
Excellence

This is to Certify that

Katherine Alexandra Cartwright

Has Achieved the Highest Standard in

Art

at Park St Public El...

Ploser Plant gan Eifion Wy...

Dewch i chwarae Ni gawn eis...

Yn y coed —

Dyna bleser Bob un ...

Plant ...

Back to school

The Coal House children had a bit of a shock when they started school back in 1927. Though their schoolmaster, Mr Michaels, was generally kind to them, he expected high standards of behaviour and presentation.

The children found their curriculum rather different too. In elementary schools (which children attended up to the school-leaving age of fourteen), a great deal of time was spent mastering multiplication facts and chanting tables of weights and measures which meant very little to them. Whilst pupils would have been familiar with pounds and ounces, inches, feet and yards in their daily lives, not many would have any practical reason for coming into contact with gills or furlongs!

At least Gwen and her friends had the opportunity to use old-fashioned money outside school as well as in the classroom. With no such things as credit or debit cards, people handled money every day – if they had any, of course. The system of pounds, shillings and pence formed the basis of arithmetic lessons at school where pupils had to convert pounds to farthings and vice versa. It was hard for the Coal House children, even the mathematically minded, to get used to adding up and subtracting in units of four and twelve and twenty, rather than in tens and hundreds.

The coins people had then would have featured either Queen Victoria's head or that of Edward VII. A new currency was issued in 1927 which had to be approved by King George V. It appeared officially on 3 November – the day that Gwen Cartwright was learning 'In Flanders Fields' at school – and no doubt copying it out in her best handwriting.

Handwriting was far more ornate than it is today, and many hours were spent practising copperplate handwriting with its elaborate curls and flourishes.

24 October 1927

Saturday today and no school

so I got up at 8.30 and had some apples and raisins for breakfast. This morning the butcher called. Mum bought a boiling chicken for Sunday lunch, and some lamb to make a shepherd's pie.

We made some parsnip and apple soup and wanted to mash the vegetables up so the soup would be smooth. We had no masher so we used the mincer instead! When we finished mincing the veggies, we went on to mince the lamb. Then we made some unleavened (flat) bread to have with our soup as we've run out of normal bread and the grocer doesn't come until tomorrow.

Using the mincer

Steph and Richie's mums arrived as a surprise but Steph was quite worried because she hasn't got very much food.

In the evening we realised there were only nine chickens instead of ten, so one has gone missing! We checked off their names. I've put the owners in brackets:

Baby (me)   Scarlet (Kitty – she's got two!)
Lady (Kitty)   Goldeneye (Angharad and Katie)
Osprey (Steffan)   Rhodri (Rhodri – confusingly!)
                             Chocolate Éclair (Gethin)

The others don't have names as we can't catch them so it must be one of those that is missing. At least it wasn't on our watch because we're looking after the pigs at the moment.

25 October 1927

Today it's Sunday (in Coal House time)

so we've got to go to church (chapel). Mum and Dad had porridge for breakfast but Dad finally relented and let me and Kitty have the last of the bread. We don't know what we'll eat for dinner tonight. We put our lunch on to cook before going to chapel. Mum fried the chicken first, which made a lovely smell. Then she added onions, carrots, swede and some rosemary and put it onto the fire to cook while we were out.

Today the minister talked about cleanliness being next to godliness and we all gave each other worried looks. (We're finding it really hard to keep clean.) And about how the Lord gives and the Lord takes away. We listened to a reading from the Old Testament (Joel: Chapter 1)

Sunday School

Chicken dinner

which was upsetting because all the sheep died. After the reading we sang some hymns: 'Calon Lân' and 'Blessed Assurance', which we had learnt in school.

There were lots of older people in the church but there weren't any other kids to come with us to Sunday School. We read a psalm, Number 21, about where to look to find God. It really means that God is everywhere and anywhere and very powerful; the posh words are 'omniscient' and 'omnipotent'. We sang 'Blessed Assurance' again and then the minister wrote some questions on the board and we wrote them down in our Sunday School books for homework.

When we got home we were disappointed to see no smoke coming out of our chimney and rushed inside to find that, actually, our fire hadn't gone out and the chicken was boiling away. Mum cooked the last potatoes from our sack and we sat down and ate! It was

absolutely delicious. We were going to have the last orange for afters but we were too full.

In the afternoon Mum did a sneaky bit of sock washing even though it's Sunday, the day of rest, and you're not really supposed to do anything. Me and Kitty did our English essays on Nelson. I had a lot to say about him and wrote on every single line.

Then, because it's Halloween tomorrow (well, it is for us even though the date is wrong), we started making our costumes. Kitty and Angharad and Katie are going to be a joint ghost with scary eyes. Daniel is going to be a zombie, Rhodri a werewolf, Gethin a mummy (his chickenpox is much better) and I'm going to be a sort of corpse bride. I made my train and then we put Rhodri in the ghost sheet and swung him about. He loved it!

After tea we played Coal House Cluedo in the dark. Cool!

26 October 1927

The baker's boy (Owain) delivered a loaf yesterday

so we had bread and honey for breakfast. I like honey!

Today Angharad didn't come to school because she's got an upset stomach. In the morning we did some science: atoms. The heaviest atom is uranium and the lightest is hydrogen. Then, after break, we painted Halloween masks. My mask is a corpse bride and Kitty's is a witch. Katie Phillips painted a werewolf for Rhodri's mask. Dan and Gethin did evil spirits.

When we went home for lunch, I had fresh bread and new cheese, which was delicious. There was time to help Mum make swede-o-lanterns (as there are no

The corpse bride

pumpkins) and when Halloween is over they can go in a stew.

Back at school we did history and learnt more about the Battle of the Somme. We had five minutes for break, instead of fifteen minutes, and then we had singing and learnt the second verse of 'Ar Hyd y Nos'.

O mor siriol gwena seren
Ar hyd y nos,
I oleuo'i chwaer ddaearen
Ar hyd y nos.
Nos yw henaint pan ddaw cystudd,
Ond i harddu dyn a'i hwyrddydd
Rhown ein golau gwan i'n gilydd
Ar hyd y nos.

Kitty's witch

Once we started singing it without the words in front of us, Kitty kept making the same mistake until Mr Whitcombe explained: 'It's "Pan ddaw cystudd" not "Pan of custard".' We also rehearsed the hymns for chapel: 'Blessed Assurance' and 'What a Friend we have in Jesus'.

We came home from school and at seven o'clock the miners still weren't back from the pit. The mums were really worried but, as it was late, they gave us our dinner and we got changed into our costumes. We did our Halloween play minus Angharad (who is still ill).

Afterwards, Mum surprised us all by bringing out fudge and hokey-pokey (a sort of toffee) – delicious! It's 9.20 as I'm writing this and the men have only just got home. There was an incident at the mine where the roof collapsed and they had to pull a man with broken legs out of the wreckage. But, then they went to the pub!

This has made me sad because they knew it was Halloween and we'd made a show, yet they didn't come home. We're doing Halloween again tomorrow because we want them to see our play and we've still got some fudge left. Yum!

Mum's Fudge Recipe

3½ oz butter

3½ oz dark brown sugar

1 can of condensed milk

Place the butter and the sugar in a saucepan, stirring until the butter melts and the sugar dissolves. Add the condensed milk and bring to the boil, stirring continuously until thick. Put in a greased tin and then chill.

The British Gazette

Published by His Majesty's Stationery Office.

No. 1. LONDON, WEDNESDAY, MAY 5, 1926. ONE PEN

FIRST DAY OF GREAT STRIKE

Not So Complete as Hoped by its Promoters

PREMIER'S AUDIENCE OF THE KING

Miners and the General Council Meet at House of Commons

FOOD SUPPLIES

No Hoarding: A Fair Share for Everybody

HOLD-UP OF THE NATION

Government and the Challenge

NO FLINCHING

The Constitution or a Soviet

COMMUNIST LEADER ARRESTED

Mr. Saklatvala, M.P., Charged at Bow Street

SEQUEL TO MAY DAY SPEECH

THE "BRITISH GAZETTE" AND ITS OBJECTS

Reply to Strike Makers' Plan to Paralyse Public Opinion

REAL MEANING OF THE ST

Conflict Between Trade Union L and Parliament

Bill for Miners Tools

1 Sledgehammer
1 Boring Rod
1 Saw
1 Shovel   £2/0/0
1 Hatchet
1 Mandrill
1 Lamp

To be paid in weekly installments before the November 1927

'TILLERY DRIFT MINE

October 1927

Men and Bosses

Today the valleys of south Wales show little evidence of the deep coal mines which dominated the landscape during the first three quarters of the twentieth century. The mining gear and the slag heaps have disappeared, leaving only rows of workers' cottages to show how important coal once was.

The coal industry in Wales was at its peak before the First World War, but by 1927 it was already in decline. Very cheap or even 'free' German coal was part of the post-war settlement with Italy and France. This meant that it was hard to sell British coal, and stoppages, pit closures and redundancies were common as a result.

The problems of the coal industry led to the first ever General Strike in May 1926. The mine owners still needed to make a profit even though the price of coal was falling. Their solution was to increase the men's working hours and cut their wages. For a while the government postponed this move, by paying the mine owners a subsidy. When the government

decided that the subsidy could no longer be paid, the miners had a tough choice: they could either accept longer hours and lower wages or face being 'locked out' of their place of work. They therefore turned to other workers for support in taking industrial action and so the General Strike was born.

Although the Strike lasted for only nine days at the beginning of May, the miners didn't go back to work, with reduced wages, until the end of the year. They and their families suffered terrible poverty as a result. Although families were grateful for help, they hated being dependent on other people's charity and no doubt the gift of cawl received by the Cartwrights would have left a bitter aftertaste.

Conditions of work underground were dirty and difficult, and accidents frequent. (The powerful headlamps worn by Joe, Cerdin and Richie were not available to miners in 1927.) Men had to pay for their own tools and walked long distances to the pit, sometimes only to find that the gates were locked and no work available.

27 October 1927

Today we had to go and watch Dad play rugby

We went along to a field where it was 'stripes' versus 'whites'. The three dads were on the whites team. They changed and then warmed up. In the first half the whites scored two tries and converted them both. Cerdin converted the second one and we all went crazy!

In the second half they scored another converted try. The stripes scored two tries but only one was converted. Dad took ages to get up from a tackle, which made us all laugh. Richie, at the end, did a back-flip because they'd won. It was really good fun.

We had bread and cheese and chutney for lunch. Afterwards we had to go to school even though it's

Joe, Cerdin and Richie

Saturday in the world outside Coal House! We did maths: Mr Michaels gave us compasses and we drew some circles and daisy patterns, and then we learnt how to draw equilateral triangles. Mr Michaels got very cross when we did square numbers because Daniel, Katie and Gethin didn't know what five times five is. He had such a shout at them and he's never usually like that. He says they've got to know their tables by tomorrow.

We went home to find out that there's no work for Dad at the mine. Nor for Ryan and Steffan. The managers only had money for two more jobs: they promoted Richie and said he could have someone else to work with him. Richie kept Cerdin's job because Dad told him that we could try and manage without wages for a bit. With Angharad ill, Debra needs Cerdin to be bringing in money.

A man came round with ferrets so the dads went out ferreting to try and catch rabbits for dinner. They didn't

Not a happy bunny

bring any back even after hours of sitting around. So, in true 'Blue Peter' style, the man with the ferrets gave us some rabbits he'd caught earlier.

They looked so cute – even though they were dead, I wanted to keep them as cuddly toys but they would soon start to rot. It's going to be quite a challenge to have to eat one.

Because Dad isn't working, he doesn't need to have meat for dinner every night so we had potato and onion omelette, which was yummy. Afterwards we each had one piece of fudge and a quarter of an apple. We've still got lots as we bought some to play bobbing apples – before Mum said that it would be too much of a waste and that the apples had to last a week. We played cards and I started teaching Katie how to play chess. She got the hang of it really quickly.

28 October 1927

Today I got up at 8.00

(but really it was 9.00 because last night the clocks went back). We had porridge for breakfast and I ate a lot of it but not all! We didn't have enough bread for Kitty's breakfast so she didn't have anything.

Before school when I was feeding the pigs, I slipped over in my just-cleaned clothes and got mud all over myself. I had to put my dirty clothes back on to go to school. Mum knew it was an accident but she was still upset as washing clothes is seriously hard work.

Last night Mr Michaels and Debra had a disagreement about him being mean to Gethin over the times tables in school yesterday. Gethin got really upset and sat crying in the coal shed for an hour. (He knows his tables in Welsh but can't remember them in English.)

DRY MEASURES

2 pints	=	1 quart
8 quarts	=	1 peck
4 pecks	=	1 bushel
8 bushels	=	1 quarter

LIQUID MEASURES

5 fluid ounces	=	1 gill
4 gills	=	1 pint
2 pints	=	1 quart
4 quarts	=	1 gallon
2 gallons	=	1 peck

Today we did science and learnt about why a clock or watch ticks. Then we did maths and learnt about liquid and dry capacity. I found having both quarts and quarters really confusing.

We came home by 10.00 because our teacher was ill. Kitty and I helped Mum make bread. I love the smell of it fresh from the oven. Mum and I ate our bread for lunch but Kitty wasn't at our house, because she was helping at Steph's. We didn't call her and she didn't know about lunch until we were halfway through it. Afterwards Mum did some knitting – she's nearly finished some mittens.

The butcher came and we traded one of dad's paintings of the cottages for loads of bacon and some liver. Nobody else likes liver but Dad does!

We went back to school in the afternoon because Sir felt better. In English we learnt about addressing

5 fluid ounces

envelopes and writing a formal letter. At break, we played 'Ice Cream' (where you have to creep up behind the person who's 'on it').

Then, when we came home, we did our Halloween concert for the men but none of them could be bothered to watch it, so we stopped and wouldn't let them see it.

For dinner Dad cooked liver, bacon and onions. I refused the liver so just had bacon and onions.

All the boys and men came round for choir practice. Then me, Dad, Cerdin, Ryan and Steffan played Fish, and Cerdin (Red-hot) won though it was the very first time he'd ever played it. Then me, Kitty, Ryan and Steffan played some more card games. I didn't win once.

We're over halfway through our time in 1927.

29 October 1927

Today I got up at 8.00. Bread for breakfast again

The Griffithses are doing the pigs and the Phillipses are doing the hens so it's our week off.

Lots happened in school today: Angharad was back in the afternoon, a girl gave me a mint, and we did lots of old-fashioned maths! In the morning we learnt about old numbers – scores, dozens and grosses – and then we did problems with old money, and inches, feet and yards.

When we went home for lunch, we found that the grocer had been but all the food had gone up in price. Bread is now one shilling instead of 5½d; it's more than doubled. (There are twelve old pence in a shilling.) Because of the

Sewing practice

way prices have gone up (the posh word is 'inflation'), Mum only bought one loaf of bread and nothing else. For lunch we ate the last home-made bread rolls.

Back in school in the afternoon the girls did childcare and the boys did technical drawing. Hmm! We learnt about bathing the baby and how good food is important and how you should have a healthy balanced diet. The girls had to embroider a button onto a handkerchief as practice for mending things.

We got home to find out that we now have a lodger. His name is Mr Mayo and he's come from the next valley to try and get work in maintenance. His wife is the fish-and-chip lady.

A little while later the rent man came in and told us that because of our lodger, the rent goes up to 11s 6d. A whole two shillings more! Mum said we'd have to get

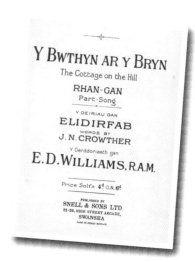

Choir practice

rid of him. Me, Kitty and the landlord were listening outside while Mum and Dad 'discussed' it. Dad overruled Mum into keeping him when she thinks it would have been easier to say no. Five shillings' rent (seven shillings minus two) is not enough to buy food for a man for a week!

Mum carried on making stew while Dad went off on a drone about the family accounts and why we should keep the lodger! For dinner, Mum chopped up the swede-o-lanterns and we had charred smily swede faces in our rabbit stew and mashed potatoes. I had stew but not the meat because it made me feel funny that a few days ago the rabbit was bouncing around in a nearby field. Daddy started singing 'Bright Eyes' which did not help!

The men went off to choir practice with our singing teacher, and I will soon be going to bed.

30 October 1927

Gunpowder, treason and plot!

In school this morning we did history – Guy Fawkes and the gunpowder plot. For lunch we had more bread and we heard the grocer had come but it was the apprentice, so Mum managed to get five shillings' worth of goods for one shilling.

Our lodger gave us some presents: tinned pineapple, chocolate and some sherbet lemons. We're going to eat the pineapple tonight and maybe even have some condensed milk with it. Mmmmmm!

In the afternoon we worked on our placards for the hunger march. Our teacher read us the story of the

Figures of authority

hunger marchers so we could choose our slogans. Mine was 'Bring Hope to the Valley'. I chose it because it has a nice ring to it and I could imagine it being chanted, so we all started chanting! Mr Michaels told us to stop because they wouldn't have done that in 1927. I painted the background red but then I stopped because it was 4.20, time to go home. TGI Friday!

We got home to find everyone in Stack Square was very clean because they had all had a bath! For dinner we had bacon, leek and potato stir fry with cheese on top. It is my favourite meal so far. Me and Kitty argued about whether to make Welsh cakes or Tinker's cakes but Welsh cakes were chosen as they don't use butter. Butter is really, really expensive whereas lard (pig fat) is pretty cheap. Me and Kitty, Ryan and Steffan played cards in the evening.

31 October 1927

Today it's saturday and I got up late!

I had toast for breakfast with butter and honey.

In the morning we made Mr Guy because we're having our Bonfire Night tonight. He's got a really good face: a sack with holes in it for eyes, nose and a mouth. And then we dressed him up in rags. We called him Mr Blandford after the mine manager. When we were about to start doing Mrs Guy, the men went up to build the bonfire and the butcher called. He only brought bacon to sell, but with him came the man to kill the chickens. Me and Kitty got so upset about killing the hens, who have come through everything with us, that we cried.

Plucking Scarlet

I made sure Baby, my chicken, was safe but somebody let them all out of the feed shed. I thought we had them all in safely so I handed one over for Mum to kill. It turned out to be Scarlet, Kitty's first chicken (before she had Lady). She got really upset and sat crying indoors until the mums decided to gut the chickens in our house. The other hen to get killed was Rhodri. Debra's had lots of partially-formed eggs in it – so not a good choice! I was fine once the chickens were dead and I helped Mum pluck ours.

Bonfire Night was really cool. I had loads of free food, like jacket potatoes and sausages in buns, because I hadn't really eaten my dinner, rabbit stew again. We put the guys on the bonfire and then we had fireworks. They were really good until one fell off the bonfire and into the crowd. That scared us. We had a singsong and then came home.

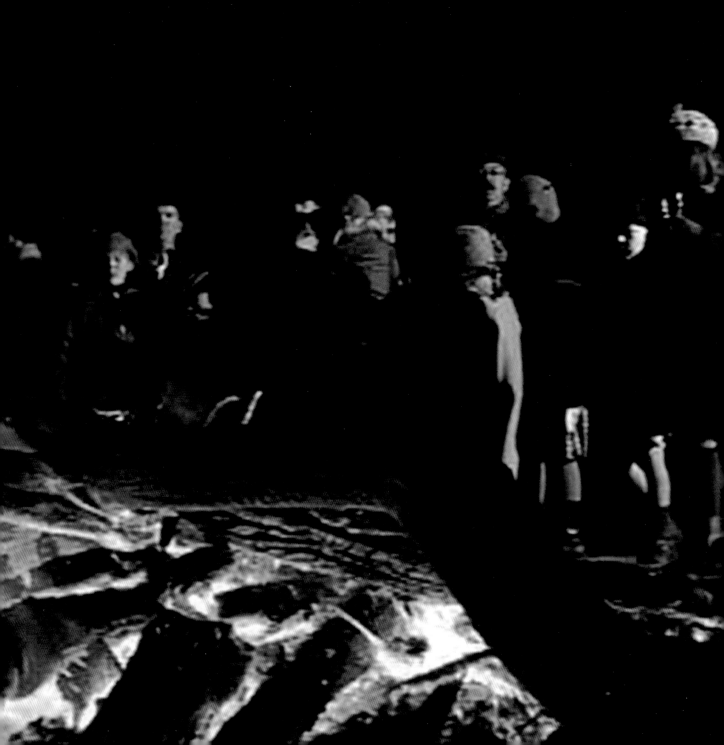

1 November 1927

I only had twenty minutes

to get dressed for chapel because I got up really late. I managed to grab some of the leftover sausage from last night and some fried jacket potatoes.

In chapel we had a prayer read by Cerdin, and Dad read the lesson. It was Luke, Chapter 10, 29–37, the story of the good Samaritan. We sang lots of hymns and then all the kids went to Sunday School. We went over our homework and luckily there were some other children there today, more than last week. The minister was thanking God for food when he asked what we were having for Sunday lunch. I replied immediately 'Scarlet'. The minister didn't know what I meant by this so he asked me what Scarlet was and I replied with a

Sunday dinner blues

straight face, 'One of our pet chickens . . .' As I said the words all the mums raised their hands to their mouths and gasped. It was very funny!

We came home for lunch. Scarlet was cooked with swede and carrots and some mashed potato. Kitty and I decided it looked so yummy we had to eat it.

In the afternoon we got out a plank and me and Rhodri played on it – like a see-saw – with Dan and Katie. Our lodger got himself locked in the toilet like I did once. It's really funny when it happens to someone else!

In the evening we had a sort of youth club and played Fish. Jade also taught us all how to play Chinese Snap. Mum and Dad went upstairs so that we could mess around downstairs. On the very last evening we're going to have a big pyjama party and eat all the leftover food! Before our youth club I made some Tinker's cakes.

Rhodri's see-saw

Tinker's Cakes

8oz flour

4oz butter

3oz sugar

4oz shredded cooking apple

Salt

Milk

Rub the butter into the flour and work in the sugar, apple and salt. Pour in a little milk and knead it into a dough. Roll out to a half-inch thickness. Bake in a heavy-bottomed frying pan for a few minutes until browned on both sides. Sprinkle with sugar and decorate with currants or any other dried fruit.

2 November 1927

Today it's Monday. School again!

For breakfast I had buttered toast with a hole in the middle! To make it, you have to put a slice of bread on a fork and hold it by the fire for five minutes on both sides. Dad managed to put the fork in upside-down so that's how he ended up making a hole.

At about seven o'clock, our door got such a banging. Mum opened it to see the mine manager, Mr Blandford, standing in the Square. He told us that all men over fourteen should be at the mine today because there's work for everyone: a new order has come in. So my dad and our lodger went off to work. The mums had a word with Mr Blandford about pithead baths and he said he'd put them in if it didn't cost him anything. The

Holy toast

mums are going to write to the MWF (Miners' Welfare Fund) for money.

At school this morning we did science and learnt about magnetism. We put a magnet under a sheet of paper and sprinkled iron filings on top and tapped it to see the effect of the magnet. We then drew the magnetic fields.

For lunch Mum made us cheese on toast. She grated the cheese because it uses less (cheese is quite expensive – 1s 6d).

In the afternoon we did art. We finished our placards by painting the letters black. I did a technique called cutting-in, by outlining the letters and then filling them in. My black paint was so thick, it was like tar. We came home from school and Mum taught me how to crochet.

Crocheting

I started crocheting a glasses-case in double and treble. It's in bluey-purple wool.

The men came home and wanted a bath so we got the hot water ready. They were going to draw straws, but then they wanted the youngest to go first, then the oldest. Eventually, everyone agreed on a running order: our lodger, Sean, then Richie, then Cerdin, then Dad. All the children had to go into the Phillipses to hide from the naked men!

After the bath was put away, we had an omelette which Mum made using our hen's eggs with fried potatoes and onions, lots of salt and pepper on top with bread and butter on the side.

It's been a busy day.

3 November 1927

Today I got up at 7.30 and had some bread for breakfast

Before we went to school, the lodger told us that because there's work everywhere in our valley, he'll be going home. I did some more crocheting and Kitty decided she wanted to learn too.

After I'd cut some squares of newspaper for toilet roll, I went outside to find Debra stamping on a pair of pants which had caught fire when they'd been drying on the range. There were two big holes in them which she had to sew up before Gethin could go to school!

Remembrance poppies

In the morning we did history and learnt a poem called 'In Flanders Fields' by John McCrae.

IN FLANDERS FIELDS the poppies blow
Between the crosses row on row,
That mark our place; and in the sky
The larks, still bravely singing, fly
Scarce heard amid the guns below.
We are the Dead. Short days ago
We lived, felt dawn, saw sunset glow,
Loved and were loved, and now we lie
In Flanders fields.

We also learnt about Armistice Day and about the poppies and the British Legion. It's so sad.

Yum!

We came home for lunch and did some revising for our maths and science exam this afternoon. For lunch I had cheese on top of scrambled egg on toast. With lots of salt and pepper. The butcher came and Mum bought stewing lamb and the butcher gave everyone some liver for free.

We went back to school and did our English exam. It was one-and-a-half hours long. It was quite difficult because it was very weirdly worded. I was the only one who managed thirty lines in my essay. The exams are important because the results will decide who can go to the County School or not. We came home and played outside. We had lamb stew and bread for dinner and there is still some left for tomorrow. We had the last of the chocolate that the lodger gave us.

All Work and No Play . . .

There was no shortage of laughter in Stack Square when all the children got together. There were no costly toys or electronic gadgets so all the fun had to be home-made. Card games and chess allowed the children to pit their wits and skill against each other and sometimes the adults joined in as well. Invented games like 'Coal House Cluedo' gave hours of pleasure to the Cartwright family and 'Hunt the Eggs' was enjoyed even by the youngest children, especially Rhodri. All the children took a great deal of mischievous delight in teasing the pigs with piggy sticks, and Rhodri found no difficulty in improvising with his wooden gun. Even a simple wooden beam was enjoyed, whether as a see-saw or a pirate's plank.

Reading was popular and Gwen would have had great enjoyment from her prize book. Dark evenings, though, and physical tiredness meant that people tended to go to bed earlier than today. Children would be tired by their walk to and from school four times a day in the fresh air and by energetic pastimes like skipping and football as well as yard games like Granny's Footsteps (what Gwen knew as 'Ice Cream' in 2007).

Both boys and girls would also have had fun helping with some of the chores, such as feeding the pigs and cleaning out the chickens. No doubt games like Cat's Cradle, greatly enjoyed by Gwen and Kitty, also helped to develop the skill and dexterity needed for household tasks like knitting and crocheting.

Best of all, perhaps, were the sing-songs around the piano, practising for concerts and performances, whether Sunday by Sunday in the chapel, or for special events such as the Cymanfa Ganu or singing festival. The concert at the end of Gwen's time in Stack Square was the highlight of her visit.

4 November 1927

Today we had a half day at school

but made it up in the afternoon by doing the maths and science exam.

In the morning we let the pigs out for about three hours. Then all of us girls – me, Jade, Kitty and Angharad – made poppies because the British Legion lady wants us to. We used red and green materials and black buttons. It took all morning and then we made some Welsh cakes! Then I made a pom-pom to go on Mum's hat. Rhodri loved it so I started making a blue one for him.

For lunch we had cheese on toast with KETCHUP! Yes! We went to school in the afternoon and did our maths and science exam. Another one-and-a-half hours. My

Hindsight

favourite question was: 'In a congregation eleven twenty-thirds are women, two thirds of the remainder are men and the rest – twenty in total – are children. How many people are at the congregation? See if you can work it out.* Kitty realised she'd got a question wrong five minutes after the end of the exam.

Just before hometime we had a look at a Davy lamp and found out why it was so important to the safety of the miners.

When I got home, I had an apple and then I went outside to play. For dinner I had leftover stew. Dad had some liver, and me and Mum tried some. It was OK but I didn't want any more.

* The answer is on page 140.

5 November 1927

Today I got up at a reasonable time

but Kitty wasn't up until half an hour before school! For breakfast I had toast and honey. Yum. Mum's making us some Welsh cakes for when we come back from school with our exam results.

When we got there, our teacher decided not to tell us our results today because he hasn't fixed the pass mark. We did some maths and went over the questions that everybody found most hard and Sir found a mistake in my science paper. I put negative neutrons instead of neutral neutrons. Whoops!

We practised singing, including 'Ar Hyd y Nos'. Angharad and I have started learning a harmony but

Making electricity

none of the others will stick to the tune and they end up singing our bit.

We came home for lunch and found out that the butcher hadn't been. Mum was making Welsh cakes and poppies. When the butcher finally arrived, he had no meat and said he'd have to take one of our pigs because there's no meat at the butcher's shop at all. We said for him to take Pepper.

Poor Ryan and Steffan (Pepper was their pig) but we've still got Salt. We loaded Pepper onto the cart and the pigs started squealing at each other.

In the afternoon at school we did some more work with magnetism, making electricity using a galvanometer and a wire coil. Then we did handwriting and learnt how to do copperplate which has lots of flourishes! We came home and did some poppies and ate lots of Welsh

Handwriting, the old fashioned way

cakes. Mum made some stewed apples and Owain the baker's boy gave some bread to Steph and some sugared almonds to me. I ate the 'sugared' but not the almonds!

We made some wood into a pirate plank. Rhodri spent all afternoon playing on it and made a flag to put on the mast of his pirate ship. For dinner we had salmon and mashed potato. I don't like salmon so I just had cheesy mash and carrots.

6 November 1927

Today I thought we were going to get our exam results at last!

I got up at 7.30 and had some toast with honey for breakfast. Dad went to work and Mum wrote a poem about our stay in the Coal House.

Coal House Thoughts

Oh, to be in Stack Square

Now November's there.

And whoever wakes in Stack Square

Finds some morning, unaware,

Steph at the pump

That the ironworks glow in the rosy light
And the frosty grass is crumbly white
While rackety jackdaws wheel in flight
In Stack Square now.

A woman's day begins,
The stove to tend.
The washing, cooking, cleaning,
Clothes to mend.
Forever on your feet,
Your hands so sore
As soon as one job's finished,
Plenty more.

Yet small delights and triumphs
Filled our days:

A fire gone out that's
Suddenly ablaze,
A scrumptious Sunday chicken,
A nice clean blouse,
The sound of children
Singing round the house,
The smell of home-made cakes!
Far dearer these
Than iPods, mobile phones and DVDs.

We went to school but Mr Michaels told us he wouldn't be giving us our results until the afternoon. We did some exam corrections in maths. It's really frustrating because you can't remember if you got the answer right or not and by the end of the lesson I was convinced that I had got everything wrong. Kitty, meanwhile, was as confident as ever. After break we finished our

An anxious moment

placards for tomorrow's concert by sticking the paper onto a board with a stick. I made another placard which Mr Michaels will be using.

We came home for lunch – a sandwich and some apple – and Mum was all eager to know our scores but we still didn't have them. It was really nerve-racking. I needed to know!

We went back to school and Mr Michaels finally gave us our results. He told me mine last just to make me feel worse. Angharad is allowed a maths re-sit because she got 85% in her English, fifth in the county, but she'd been away for so much of the arithmetic. Kitty also suffered in the maths. The overall pass mark was an average of 70 plus. Kitty got 61% in maths and 73% in English, an average of 67%. But she has got a referral on Wednesday at 2.00, which means a meeting with the head of the school. I got 84% in maths and 93% in

Results

English so I am through to the County School! I wonder if this really had been 1927 whether I would have been able to go. The uniform would have been very expensive and we might not have been able to afford it. I would probably have gone into service as a maid somewhere. Especially if Dad kept on hurting himself!

We came home and told Mum our marks. She had made some fudge so Kitty and I had some. Kitty got a bit upset about her results because she thought she could have done better. We had boiled ham with loads of veggies for dinner, which was delicious.

We all played cards in the evening and had lots of fun. Then Ryan and Steffan started trying to fire a huge log out of their bows and arrows. It was really funny!

7 November 1927

Last night we went to bed really late

because we thought there was no school today – but there was!

I got up at 8.00, thinking I had plenty of time for breakfast (bread that was almost toasted with some butter and honey) and then found out we had to go to school (even though it's Saturday in the Coal House!), all because of the Cymanfa Ganu or singing festival this evening. We practised doing our two songs: 'Ar Hyd y Nos' and the first verse of 'Blessed Assurance' and also a poem by Eifion Wyn called 'Pleser Plant'.

It must be playtime soon

Pleser Plant

Dewch i chwarae
Yn y coed.
Dyna bleser
Plant erioed.

Ni gawn eistedd
Bob yn ail
Rhwng y blodau
Mân a'r dail.

A dod adre
Cyn yr hwyr
Wedi blino
Mam a ŵyr.

Byr yw diwrnod
Plentyn bach.
Rhaid yw chwarae
Os yn iach.

We went through everything in the concert and then we went outside for break and did some skipping games. When we went back in, we practised our copperplate handwriting. We did some more singing and learnt the 'Ash Grove' even though it wasn't in the concert.

When we came home, Mum immediately set about my very greasy hair with a bar of pink soap. She washed it and put it up in a turban. She had made some fudge while we'd been at school. We'd had quite a lot of it before Mum told us to stop.

For lunch she cooked sausages with onion gravy, mash

Male voice choir

and carrots and swede. We were expecting Dad home between 1.30 and 2.00. But at 2.30 he still wasn't home so we had lunch without him. Yum! We spent all afternoon worrying about the concert and eating fudge. We had some sausage rolls for dinner and then I changed into my Sunday best. I had to wait until after eating to put it on in case of spillages.

Dad went off to the concert before the rest of us to have a quick rehearsal with the choir. Half an hour later we followed. Everyone from school went backstage and ran through the harmony with our singing teacher who is also the choir master. Then we went and sat in the audience.

The male voice choir sang 'Laudamus' which was so beautiful. Everybody sang a few hymns and then it was us! I nearly wet myself with 'nervitement', a cross between nervousness and excitement. We did our poem and remembered all the words! Everyone clapped. Then

Cymanfa Ganu

we sang 'Ar Hyd y Nos'. It was beautiful and Debra started crying. Our harmony went really well and we got a huge round of applause.

We sat down and everyone sang a few more hymns like 'Calon Lân'. Then Mum, Debra and Stephie performed their poems. Stephie went first and her poem about Rhodri was really sweet. Then Debra did hers – it sounded a good poem but I didn't understand it because she did it in Welsh. Mum recited her poem which really rounded off the other two.

Then it was the school prize-giving. There were prizes for lots of different subjects. Here is a list of the winners:

Art	Kitty
History	Daniel
Welsh	Gethin

Bedtime reading

Junior Maths	Katie
English	Angharad
Maths	Gwen!

I won the certificate for maths! Then the tension started to build up for the presentation of the book for the best pupil. Mr Michaels began to describe his reasons for awarding the prize, but we still weren't able to guess who the winner was. Then he called out my name! The smile on my face when I shook hands with Mr Blandford, the mine manager, was so huge it could have swallowed a whale.

After all the women and girls had sung 'Amazing Grace', we finally came home. It was all over. We have one more day and then we will leave, never coming back.

8 November 1927

Today was our last full day and night in the coal house

After breakfast – bread and butter – we started packing up everything we wanted to take, like our schoolwork and our piano music.

Then we cleared out the food cupboard, except for the things we wanted for dinner. We gave it all to Salt, the remaining pig! Jade gave her a whole jar of honey and we gave her half a loaf of Bara Brith. Surprisingly, it was the Bara Brith and honey she ate, even though she was surrounded by mounds of vegetables and potatoes.

A game of cards

Mum decided it would be a good idea to cook up all the leftover ingredients like sugar, flour and butter. We made loads of Welsh cakes and Tinker's cakes and fudge to eat at our big pyjama party! At the party we're also going to play Fish – a big hit – and Chinese Snap. Chinese Snap is really good for playing with lots of people. Jade is amazing at it, but so she should be as she taught us how to play it.

After a lunch of <u>more</u> bread we carried on with our packing. We had two great big sacks and it was really sad putting all our precious things and memorabilia into them. It was fun seeing all the things and going 'Oooooh, there's my Halloween mask, isn't it scary?' Yet at the same time it was pretty sad. I put in about a year's supply of raisins. Honey and raisins are the two things I've started to like most in the past four weeks. The two things I've missed the most are . . . Tomato Ketchup and Frozen Peas! Dried peas are <u>really</u> weird.

Time for bed

Mum started cooking the bits of Pepper we bought from the butcher this morning. Pork chops! She cooked them with apples and parsnips and when we ate them they were absolutely delicious!

Afterwards Mum and Dad went upstairs as the kids took over the ground floor. We ate everything and played game after game of Fish and Chinese Snap. At about nine o'clock, we all decided to go to bed for the very last time in 1927, preparing for the early start tomorrow.

9 November 1927

Last ever day in the Coal House!

And I'm a bit lost for words. I had eggs for my last ever meal cooked on Mr O'Brien. I wore my pinnie and apron to do the chores for the last ever time. The children – all of us – fed Salt (the pig) and the chickens. We went through all the stuff packed into the sacks, checking we had everything. It was really strange, looking at what had happened to us and what we'd all been through together, but then realising that we would be leaving it all in a few hours.

I went outside and sat on a wall looking over the ironworks. I felt like I was saying goodbye to a really good friend. I knew that I would never be back here in the same way. But these four weeks will always have a special place in my heart.

Goodbye

Children playing outside in the mud, laughing, smiling.

Oh, the food! Some nice, some disgusting!

All modern luxuries gone, yet more joyful than ever.

Laughter, not riches, built our lives inside this house.

Having fun, playing with everyone!

Our time spent together, we've learnt life's true values.

Understanding our past sent us all on this mission, but,

Somehow we've learnt more about the present and future.

Everyone sticks together,

Community spirit,

  Atmosphere,

    Coal house.

       Gwen

Gwen Cartwright
Former resident of Number 7 Stack Square

Epilogue

It has now been eight months since I last exited Number 7, dressed in 1927 clothes. I have no regrets, and I would do it again if the opportunity was offered.

I have been back to Stack Square and always feel very nostalgic. The pig and chickens are no longer there and all our things have gone but it still feels very special.

And if I listen very closely I can almost hear Stephie at the pump, Debra laughing and the sound of children playing in the yard.

Who's who?

1. Annabel
2. Gwen
3. Kitty
4. Gethin
5. Daniel
6. Katie
7. Gwennan
8. Steph
9. Jade
10. Ryan
11. Steffan
12. Angharad
13. Debra
14. Joe
15. Cerdin
16. Richie
17. Rhodri

* The answer to the question on page 110 is 115: there are 55 women, 40 men and 20 children.

Acknowledgements

This diary would not have been possible without the constant support of my family and friends: my sister Kitty, who was there throughout the experience; my dad, who, although grumpy at times, kept me going; and of course, very special thanks to my mum – without you this diary would still be a dream in a notebook. I love you dearly.

Gwen Cartwright

The author and publishers would like to thank the following: BBC Wales; Staff at Indus Films for advice and support; Cadw, Welsh Assembly Government, for permission to take photographs at Blaenavon Ironworks; Staff at Blaenavon Ironworks for their practical help.

The author and publishers would like to thank the following for permission to reproduce photographs in this volume:

Ray Edgar: i, ii, iv (top left, centre left, centre, upper centre right), 6, 7, 8, 10, 11, 13, 14, 20, 26, 30, 40 (4), 41 (centre), 46, 48, 50, 52, 56 (bottom right), 58, 65, 66, 71, 78, 81, 82, 86, 89, 94, 98, 100, 101,102, 105, 106 (top centre, top right, bottom), 108, 112, 115 (centre), 116, 122, 125, 128, 130, 133, 134, 137, 138, 143, 144.

Brian Griffiths: 42.

John Hunter: 73, 76.

Patrick Olner: iv (bottom left, top middle); 35, 62, 107 (centre), 111, 129, 141, cover filmstrip (centre photograph).

Mei Williams: 36, 39, 45, 51, 61, 90, 97, 106, 107 (top right), 139.

Indus Films: stills iv (top right, lower centre right, bottom centre, bottom right), 6 (inset), 7 (inset left & right), 12, 16, 17, 18, 22, 23 (2), 24 (left), 28 (2), 32, 33, 38 (2), 41 (top), 44, 55, 56 (bottom left), 57 (2), 60, 64 (2), 65, 72 (bottom), 77, 85, 88, 92, 93, 96, 109, 110, 118, 119, 120, 121, 124, 126,127, 132, 137.

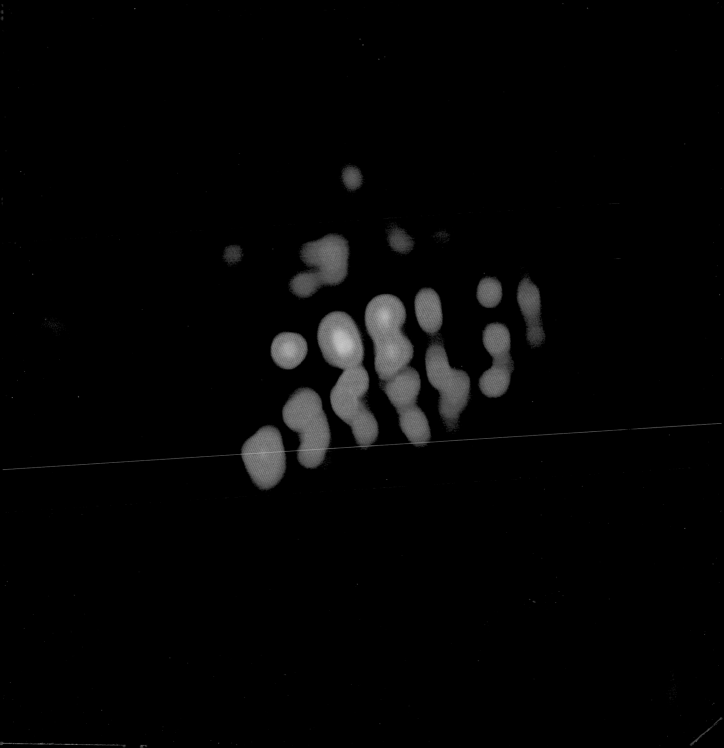